CHIEF STORYTELLING OFFICER

More tales
From
America's
Foremost
Corporate
Storyteller

David Armstrong

© Copyright 2002

Chief Storytelling Officer

© 2002 by David Armstrong

www.ARMSTRONG-INTL.COM

Book cover design and photography by Kurt Armstrong

ISBN 0-9648027-6-7

© 2002 by David Armstrong

All Rights Reserved

Printed in the United States of America

September 2002

10,9,8,7,6,5,4,3,2,1

Stories to Enjoy

I.	**STORIES TO KICK-START *URGENCY***		
	1.	Hear Etta Page, See Grant Run	1
	2.	Ice Cream Bars	3
	3.	Adam Andretti	6
II.	**STORIES TO MAKE PEOPLE *BRAVE AND WISE***		
	4.	Armstrong Cleaners, Inc.	11
	5.	Cellular Phones	15
	6.	Harold Coop, Inc.	17
	7.	Cupid's Arrow	19
	8.	The Ten Dollar Doctor Visit	21
	9.	It's Your Fault	25
III.	**STORIES TO TURN US INTO *CHANGE GOURMETS***		
	10.	Tie Day	29
	11.	Please Remember Me	32
	12.	Heinz	35

STORIES TO ENJOY

IV.	STORIES ABOUT HAVING *FUN*	
	13. Armstrong's Fire Department	41
	14. A Piece Of Fun	44
	15. Nicole's Crayons	46
	16. Look...It's The Blimp	49
	17. Be Kind To Animals	52
	18. Court Jester	55
	19. Let's Make An Armstrong Deal	59
V.	STORIES TO GET PEOPLE TO *COMMUNICATE* ABOUT THINGS WORTH *COMMUNICATING* ABOUT	
	20. The Problem With Plant Tours	67
	21. Do You Speak English?	70
	22. Target Practice	73
	23. Voice Mail	76
	24. I Found A Message In A Bottle	78
	25. Slam	81
	26. Man's Best Friend	83
	27. They're Great!!! ®	86

STORIES TO ENJOY

VI. STORIES ABOUT *CORE VALUES*
28.	A Born Again Christian	91
29.	R.H.I.P	94
30.	Let's Pray	96
31.	Dear Friend	98
32.	Guardian Angel	100

VII. STORIES TO BOOST *CREATIVITY*
33.	Grandpa's Gift	111
34.	A Horse Thief	114
35.	R.I.P.	117
36.	Color Inside The Lines	120

VIII. STORIES TO HONOR *PARTNERSHIPS*
37.	Clankety Clank! Clankety Clank!	125
38.	Lauren's First Visit With Santa	127
39.	Twins	129
40.	Bowling In England	131
41.	A Penny	133

STORIES TO ENJOY

IX.	**STORIES TO HONOR *QUALITY AND SERVICE***	
	42. If You Build It, You Will Buy It!	139
	43. Vent Wire	142
	44. Valentines Day	144
	45. Ed Kirchner's Secret	146

X.	**STORIES TO INSPIRE *INNOVATION***	
	46. Top Secret	151
	47. Manifolds	155
	48. The Vote	157
	49. Baby's First Christmas!	160

XI.	**STORIES TO MAKE EVERYONE A *LEADER***	
	50. Dull Crayons	167
	51. Kick Me	169
	52. Ex-Patriot	172
	53. Armstrong's Michelangelo	174
	54. One Hundred Dollars	177
	55. Your Yearly Performance Review	180

Stories To Enjoy

XII.	**STORIES ABOUT FINDING NEW SOURCES OF *PROFIT***	
	56. The Death Of A Sick Armstrong Product	185
	57. $48.45	188
	58. A Treasure Hunt	191
	59. Camelot	193
	60. Let There Be Light	196
	61. Scrap	199
	62. Tomorrow Is Not Promised	201

XIII.	**STORIES ABOUT WHY *SMALL IS BEAUTIFUL***	
	63. The $55,000 Comb	205
	64. Pewwww!	207
	65. The Apron	209
	66. Who Parked In My Parking Space?	211

Stories To Enjoy

XIV.	**STORIES TO INSPIRE *SELF-MANAGEMENT***		
	67.	IOU's	217
	68.	Next Day Delivery	220
	69.	Director Of First Impressions	223
	70.	The Chauffer	226
	71.	Armstrong's General Store	228
XV.	**STORIES ABOUT *STORYTELLING***		
	72.	Armstrong's First Honorary Employee	235
	73.	A Voice From The Past	237
	74.	Video Story	240
	75.	Pinocchio	242
	76.	Survivors Found	244
	77.	Scout's Honor	246

Stories to Enjoy

XVI.	STORIES ABOUT *TRADITION*	
78.	911	251
79.	Like Father Like Son	253
80.	Chocolate Chip Cookies	256
81.	Armstrong Trap Magazine	258
82.	Alligator Briefcase	261

XVII.	STORIES ABOUT *LEGENDS AND TALL TALES*	
83.	Aloha	265
84.	Bill Drumm's Mortgage	268
85.	Layoff	271
86.	A Feather In Our Hat	274

Stories To Enjoy

XVIII. ARMSTRONG *FABLES*

	87.	The Goat Amongst The Sheep	280
	88.	The Foxes And The Hunter	282
	89.	The Turtle And The Fisherman	285
	90.	The Geese And Their Coffee	288
	91.	The Parrot Whispers Sadness To The Sheep	291
	92.	The Jackal And The Loyal Dog	295
	93.	The Black Colt And The Brown Colt	298
	94.	The Skunk And The Colt	301

XIX. *ROOKIE* STORYTELLERS

	95.	Another Christmas Carol	307
	96.	First Names	309
	97.	One Match Fire Making	312
	98.	A Trip To Remember	314
	99.	Armstrong Steam University	316
	100.	Finding Fault	318

SPECIAL DEDICATION:

In loving memory of my mother, Barbara Irene Armstrong. God is with you. I told a few stories in my younger days, but they were all true. Really, mom! To better understand the love and kindness my mother shared, you need to read the story, "A Trip To Remember" found in the back of this book.

ACKNOWLEDGEMENT

Time is an equal opportunity resource; no one has enough of it yet each of us have all there is. Kathy Spencer, my assistant, always seems busy, yet she makes sure she always has time for typing and proofreading these stories with a smile. This book would not have been possible without her hard work and dedication. Kathy, your patience with me compels me to honor you with acknowledgement.

FOREWORD

"All cultures, all ages, all genders, all races, all levels of experience, all levels of education, and all businesses, yesterday, today, and tomorrow, believe and enjoy storytelling."

STORIES
TO KICK-START
URGENCY

CHAPTER 1

1.
HEAR ETTA PAGE, SEE GRANT RUN

This story begins each day in the parking lot between Plant 1 and Plant 3 of Armstrong International, Inc. in Three Rivers. Throughout the day, you will find Armstrongers walking between the plants, checking on orders, moving parts, repairing machines, etc. It's not a short walk, probably 500 feet of parking lot between the two plants. To understand why we have 500 feet between the plants, you need to read my story, "Our Promise to Fred Kemp," found in Managing By Storying Around. A lot of times people ride our people movers to save time, and of course, the fork trucks are used for moving product. There are still those who like to exercise, and walk across the parking lot to the next plant. Grant Kain is one of those Armstrongers. Grant Kain has a nice steady walking pace; not too fast, not too slow, but when he hears the loudspeaker blast out, **"Grant Kain, would you please dial 322,"** he begins to run to the nearest phone.

Hear Etta page, see Grant run!!

STORIES TO KICK-START URGENCY   1

THE MORAL OF THE STORY

1. **Hear Etta page, see Grant run!**
Ed Kirchner told me this story one day. He began with, "Hear Etta page, see Grant run." Rumor has it that almost every time Etta Griffin, Grant's Secretary, pages Grant over the loud speaker, he runs to the nearest phone to answer the page. If Grant is walking between Plants 1 and 3, he still runs if he hears the page. I told Ed I didn't believe him, but Stu Warner, who heard Ed tell me the story, confirmed it.

2. **A prime function of a leader is to keep urgency alive.**
You can talk about it all you want, tell story after story, and still people love to procrastinate. When Armstrongers become uncomfortable around their leaders because they're too slow, maybe then they will speed up. More Armstrong leaders have to practice urgency, like Grant running to the phone. It works. Remember . . . Ed and Stu noticed it.

3. **Time is the currency of the future.**
Time will be more valuable than quality, **time** will be more valuable than innovation, **time** will be more valuable than service, **time** will be the key to success in business. **Time** — no one has enough of it. You save time for your customers, and they will pay you well. Grant knows this and practices it every day for all to see.

2.
ICE CREAM BARS

John Greenhalgh, President of Power Specialties, Inc., is not a common man, for he gets high on urgency. It all started in late fall 1996 when international sales for Armstrong grew by over 30%. It was very difficult for Armstrong to ship on time. To make things worse, earlier that year Armstrong had installed a new computerized manufacturing system which was still being debugged. To improve the flow of product in the factory, machines and departments had been relocated. The combination of these events created a delivery problem and a lot of customer complaints.

The year 1998 had just begun and a meeting was in progress between Armstrong International's executives and nine presidents from its representative sales force. This meeting, called **AMWREP**, is held twice a year. Deliveries had returned to normal. Once again Armstrong deliveries were the best in our industry, and many improvements had been made to simplify placing orders with the factory. The Armstrong employees had worked hard for over a year with a lot of overtime. They were tired and stressed.

John immediately stood up and said, "I think we as the representatives need to say thank you to these people. We need to reward them and let them know that we appreciate what they have done."

All the other presidents nodded in agreement, but nobody came up with a suggestion on what kind of reward to give.

John then said, "Why don't we give everybody at the factory an ice cream bar?" Nobody responded. Completely frustrated, John walked out of the meeting and placed a call to Armstrong International. He asked that ice cream bars be purchased and handed to all the employees with special thanks from the representative sales force. John requested that the bill be sent to his company, Power Specialties. Shortly thereafter, John returned to the meeting with ice cream bars in hand. He began handing them out to all the people at the meeting. To this day nobody knows where John got the ice cream bars so quickly.

Be fast, faster, fastest.

THE MORAL OF THE STORY

1. **A committee is a group of people who keep minutes and waste hours.**
John knew the idea was good. It was simple, inexpensive, and the Armstrongers needed some praise—why wait? Meetings are only as good as the actions taken—quickly taken!

2. **Simpler is faster.**
Simple things are easy to think of and easy to implement. If you want to be quick, practice the simple things—like handing out ice cream bars.

3. **Be Predictable!**

John Greenhalgh has a reputation of being impatient, and it's well-earned. <u>Everytime</u> you meet John Greenhalgh, he needs something done quickly. You want everybody to know that you are impatient. As a leader, people will come to know your reputation and will want to please you with quick action. You <u>earn</u> this reputation by demanding urgency <u>each</u> day. Be predictable like John Greenhalgh.

3.

ADAM ANDRETTI

It all ends when the checkered flag drops and a race car crosses the finish line in first place. The winner is Adam Andretti by half a car length. Adam takes his victory lap and pulls into the winner's circle. The camera zooms in on Adam and the race car. Printed on the hood of the car are the words *Cannon Downrigger* with its logo. As the camera focuses on the driver's door you see other sponsors by the names of *Bottomline FishFinder, Bottomline SideFinder, and Armstrong*. As the camera tightens in on Adam's face he talks about how exciting the race was, and how grateful he is to his family, pit crew, sponsors, and fans.

Early in the spring of 1999, Kim Sears from Affiliated Steam, headquartered in Chicago, contacted David Casterline at Armstrong International, Inc. Kim told David that Adam Andretti was looking for sponsors for his car. Kim had become a strong supporter of Adam mostly due to the fact that Adam had spent a great deal of time with Kim's son, Corey. David decided to call Adam Andretti and found himself impressed with Adam's high morals, maturity, and professionalism, not to mention his family's long reputation in the racing circuit. It didn't take long for *Bottomline®* FishFinder, *Cannon®* Downrigger, *Bottomline®* SideFinder, and *Armstrong* to become sponsors of the Andretti car.

> *If things seem under control, you're just not going fast enough.*
> —Mario Andretti

THE MORAL OF THE STORY

1. **Become obsessed with speed.**
The Andretti's are obsessed with speed. They make a great living from it. So will Armstrong International, but only if we are faster than our competition. To become faster, we must be obsessed with speed.

2. **Speed sells!**
Speed will always sell, no matter what the product or service, and no matter what century we live in. This is why Armstrong International, Inc. has chosen the vision statement **Consider it Done √.**

3. **Cultivate a culture of speed.**
Not only does Adam Andretti drive fast, his pit crew makes repairs quickly. Armstrong International, Inc. and its divisions must have the same culture. This culture starts with the leaders and is practiced by <u>all</u> employees.

4. **Spend money to become faster.**
Adam Andretti needs a fast racecar, which costs money. They continue to invest money in his racecar to maintain the winning edge. Armstrong International, Inc. and Computrol need to spend money on equipment to remain faster than their competition. We will continue to spend money to remain faster. Before you use this story in hopes of getting

me to invest in equipment to improve speed, remember that the customer must be willing to pay "more" for speed. Some times the speed we sell is an <u>illusion</u> and only benefits our employees not our customers.

STORIES
TO MAKE PEOPLE
BRAVE AND WISE

CHAPTER 2

4.

ARMSTRONG CLEANERS, INC.

Psssssh. Psssssssh. The smell of hot steam hits the air as a shirt is being pressed. In a corner of Armstrong Cleaners, Inc., a young lady takes a dress and puts it over the Suzie II Form Finisher machine which presses her dress. It is hot in the little store. The clothes are piled high, waiting to be pressed. Just then the door opens, and in walks an Armstrong employee.

"Does anybody know how to get the wrinkles out of a pair of pants?"

"Sure, I'll show you how," replied another Armstronger. "You lay the pants on the steam finishing board -- making sure they are nice and flat. Then push the lever on the all-steam iron, and press out the wrinkles."

"You mean like this?"

Pssssssh.

"Yeah, that's right."

"Wow, they look great! Thanks."

Again, the door opened, and an Armstrong employee sticks her head into the store.

"Oh, it looks pretty busy in here. When will somebody be done?"

"I'll be done in about ten minutes. Why don't you come back then?"

"I can't. My lunch hour will be over. I'll come back after work. Thanks anyway."

The lady shuts the door, takes a few steps, sits down at a table and finishes eating lunch with her fellow Armstrongers.

The ending to this story is what makes it worth telling. For you see, Armstrong Cleaners, Inc. is located inside the factory walls of Armstrong International, right next to The Armstrong Impressions Print Shop and Armstrong Post Office. Around the corner, stands the Armstrong General Store. These stores are interconnected to give the illusion of a town within the Armstrong factory. Each store serves a business purpose, whether printing literature, shipping literature, steam-pressing employee's clothes or selling gifts with the Armstrong logo.

Playing is one of the best ways to learn.

THE MORAL OF THE STORY

1. **"Play with your customer's products and become familiar with their needs."**
Bob Hradsky, Corporate Vice President/Special Projects, built a strong relationship with Cissel Manufacturing Company, the largest steam finishing equipment manufacturer in the world. So strong was this relationship that Cissel was gracious enough to donate the equipment for Armstrong Cleaners, Inc. We sell to them as an "original equipment manufacturer" (OEM). Our steam traps go on their equipment. Their equipment can be found in laundries and dry cleaners throughout the world. We can now develop new products for Cissel and test them on Cissel equipment. As we play with Armstrong Cleaners, Inc., we will become wiser about Cissel's business and will relate more closely to their problems. I think Cissel, who is

one of our better customers, will be pleased with Armstrong for becoming familiar with their equipment.

2. **Let the college students who are children of Armstrong employees press the clothes.**
"Armstrong's College Scholarship" program found in my book, <u>Managing By Storying Around</u>, works just fine — when there's work. But what do we do when we don't have enough orders? What's wrong with letting the college students press clothes? Better yet, we can help them become entrepreneurs—wise entrepreneurs. Let them service fellow Armstrongers (customers) at Armstrong International. I can see them making deliveries, taking special instructions on pressing favorite garments, managing their time, providing a quality job, dealing with irate customers and scheduling repairs to the equipment when it breaks. Our college scholarship program is designed not only to provide money to these college students, but also to teach them good work ethics, make them wiser, and to provide them with the opportunity (when possible) to do a job similar to the career they have chosen.

3. **Armstrong International, Inc. has never had a layoff, only a reduced work week after the stock market crash of October, 1929.**
We intend to keep it that way. But what do you do when there are more employees than orders? Why not staff the laundry store with one of our full-time employees? This will keep him or her busy and will provide a service or perk to other Armstrong employees and guests.

4. **I see Armstrong Cleaners, Inc. as another opportunity for an Armstrong Character.**
Just imagine having some guest visit Armstrong. During their stay, they need a shirt or a pair of slacks pressed. We take them to Armstrong Cleaners, Inc. and are greeted by an Armstrong character who is the store owner. Don't you think that would leave an impression worth remembering? Why, you ask? Because it's unusual, different and special!

5.
CELLULAR PHONES

Come with me to the windy city of Chicago. It was June 17, 1998. Tom Sparks, President of Steam Economies Company, and I were discussing his company's Pro Forma Income Statement for 1998. As we went down the list of budget items, I stopped on the item titled "Cellular Phone."

"These expenses seem very high to me, Tom."

"Last year they were even higher," replied Tom. "I've talked to my salesmen and convinced them to start watching the amount of time they use their cellular phones. It's real hard to get them to cut back."

"Why don't you eliminate the cellular phones? That will save you even more."

Tom smiles, "I thought about that and at our last sales meeting I asked the salesmen if they could do without their cell phones." They shouted, "You can't do that! Our customers won't be able to reach us!" That's when I lost it! "Didn't I tell you guys not to give your cell phone number to our customers? In the past, they called the phone number for Steam Economies Company. Now, if we do away with your cell phones, our customers won't know who to call." Tom shakes his head in disappointment.

"I never thought about that. I've got to write a memo to Armstrong Service in Orlando to make sure they don't make the same mistake. Better yet, I'll write a story."

"Good luck, David. Remember, I told my salesmen

and they still gave their cell phone number to our customers."

> *You think public pay phones are expensive, try cellular phones!*

THE MORAL OF THE STORY

1. **A secret told is a secret no more.**
I share Tom's story because we can all learn from it. You can be trapped into using cellular phones once you give the number to a customer. Don't do it! You probably will. Read moral two to know why.

2. **"He who knows others is wise, he who knows himself is enlightened"** –Lao-Tze, Chinese philosopher 604-531 B.C.
Each of us seeks to find a way to make things easier. Cellular phones are very convenient, thus addictive. You <u>will</u> overuse the cellular phone and give the number to customers. This is what Lao-Tze warned us about. Be careful how you use your cellular phone. Know yourself.

3. **"Tell me, and I'll forget; Show me, and I may remember; Involve me, and I'll understand"**– Chinese Proverb.
If your employees must have cellular phones, I recommend once a month you take the cellular phones away -- for several days. Start with the first month or you may be too late. This will scare your employees so they won't give their cellular numbers to customers. Why? Because they won't know when you're going to take away their cellular phone; only that it will be <u>often</u>. Involve me and I will understand.

6.
HAROLD COOP, INC.

Come with me as we deliver some Armstrong Steam Traps to Harold Coop, Inc. Armstrong International sub-contracts the painting of our steam traps to Harold Coop, Inc. Harold's company is very small; actually, he is the only employee. Upon entering his store, I find Harold busy at work painting steam traps. Quietly, I stand back and watch. He takes great pride in making sure that the total surface of the product is covered, being careful not to have any runs in the paint. I watch him set the spraygun down and clean it making sure it would be ready for the next job. Carefully, he places each of the products on a conveyer belt which moves them in front of two large fans, which helps dry the paint quicker.

When Harold turned around and saw me, he was startled — I could tell by his face and the size of his eyes. He pulled his mask down (now blue from the paint) and smiled.

"Hello, I didn't know you were here. How long have you been waiting?"

"Not too long, just long enough to watch you take pride in your work. You do a real nice job. Our products really look good."

"Thank you...so what can I do for you, David?"

"Well, I have been a customer of yours for a long time, as you know, and I couldn't help but notice that your store had a facelift--it really looks good."

"I'm glad you noticed, I spent a lot of time on it. I cleaned all the equipment and repainted it with bright colors to make it more cheerful for our customers."

"You really love your job don't you?"

"I sure do."

"It shows. I especially like the Armstrong logo painted on your equipment."

If you lose ownership, you lose desire.

THE MORAL OF THE STORY

1. **Let each day be your masterpiece.**
Harold is an Armstrong employee. He works in the paintbooth. No matter what job you do, be the best you can be at it. Become a master...a professional. Let your work be compared to the greatest artists, poets and composers of all time. Harold Coop is the Michelangelo for painting steam traps.

2. **Keep the entrepreneur spirit alive.**
Harold has taken his job of painting steam traps and made it into a business, a new business — a company of one. He has named it Harold Coop, Inc. Painting the equipment and adding the Armstrong logo reveals Harold's entrepreneurial spirit. A state of mind...I can make a difference.

3. **You can be a valuable brand, just like one of our products...**and how do you spell your brand? **JOB SECURITY!**

7.
CUPID'S ARROW

Just the other day, I heard one of Cupid's arrows whiz by me hitting a fellow Armstronger right in the heart. Cupid had shot two arrows that day at Armstrong International. Both Armstrong employees soon began dating. This was not the first time Cupid had visited Armstrong International.

Many years ago I recall the sorrow Cupid's arrow brought upon two Armstrongers. Both of Cupid's victims worked in the same Armstrong International division. One even reported to the other. Both were married, which came to an end after Cupid's arrow pierced their hearts. They are no longer employees of Armstrong International for reasons other than Cupid's arrow. There have been other Armstrongers whose love affair has ended bitterly. Many times these Armstrongers still have to work together, which is difficult. Their story does not end happily ever after.

When Cupid aims in the workplace — duck!

THE MORAL OF THE STORY

1. **Cupid's arrow can damage a company.**

Office love affairs that end bitterly can affect more than the two lovers. Employees take sides. It can affect all their friends at work. Productivity can go down, careless errors get made, and cooperation suffers — all because of a soured love affair.

2. **Supervisor and subordinate love affairs can be even more expensive to a company**.
When the love affair is strong, other co-workers may believe favoritism on the job exists. Don't believe that these love affairs remain a secret. Now, what if the couple has a nasty break-up? This could lead to sexual harassment.

3. **Duck Cupid's arrows**.
We are not saying employees can't date, only to be careful so that it does <u>not</u> affect your performance at work. We also ask that you be discreet.

4. **"If you have to have a policy manual, publish the Ten Commandments"–Robert Townsend, CEO Avis.**
You shall not commit adultery. God's seventh commandment found in Exodus:20. God's laws are always above man's laws.

8.

THE TEN DOLLAR DOCTOR VISIT

The Christmas holidays were nearing and I found myself in Three Rivers, Michigan. This was my third trip to hand out my new book Once Told, They're Gold, to the Armstrong employees. To personalize my book, I autograph each one with the first name of each employee. This brought me to the punch press department where I was talking with Bill Hartman.

"Bill, can you give me the employee names in your department? I want to make sure that my list is accurate."

"Hmmm, let me see, there is Larry Hagenbuch, Dave O'Dell, Fred Newbre, Roger Marks, Bob Kirchner, and David Boote."

"OK Bill, I've got all those names what about the bucket department."

"Lets see, there's Steve Hay, Keith Knisely, Kim Loomis and Roger Peters"

"Thanks, if we forgot anybody, just let me know." I opened a book and began writing, L-A-R-R-Y   H-A-G-...

"Here comes Bob Kirchner," whispers Bill. I looked up. "You are going to have to speak up. He has a problem hearing in one of his ears. He just returned from the doctor."

"Hi David."

"Hi Bob. How's the ear?"

"Oh the doctor said I have some water on it from the last time I was sick so he has me on some antibiotics. You know, that was a great experience. I haven't been to the doctor in seven years."

"Seven years!!" I repeated.

"Yeah, seven years. The new P.P.O. (Preferred Provider Organization) health plan that Armstrong started using only cost me $10.00 for the doctor visit. I also didn't have to fill out any paperwork. Talk about easy. I left at 11:10 a.m. and got back 11:45 a.m. I really like our new health insurance plan."

"Bob, you are the first person to compliment our P.P.O plan. Thanks!"

"I have some more good news," adds Bill. "My retired father told me that several of his retired friends were complaining about the cost of their health care. When asked, my father told them he had no problem because Armstrong helped cover the cost of his prescriptions."

God helps those that help themselves.
— Ben Franklin

THE MORAL OF THE STORY

1. **Armstrong's P.P.O. is only as good as those who use it.**

We made our P.P.O. health plan <u>optional</u>. Our employees have the option to continue using the current health plan or to use the new P.P.O. plan. We did this because we were concerned that some employees would be upset if they could no longer consult their family doctor. Not all doctors belong to a P.P.O. Using the P.P.O. will save you money and eliminate paperwork. Bob Kirschner, assistant foreman, helped himself by using our P.P.O. plan and only paid $10—with no paperwork.

2. **Children keep things simple, and so should Armstrong keep its health insurance plan simple.**
Remember my story titled "Lunch with the President" found in How to Turn Your Company's Parables into Profit? In moral number two of that story I explained that the forms for health insurance should be easy to fill out and the program should be easy to understand. What could be simpler than eliminating the forms? Maybe knowing you only have to pay $10 per visit.

3. **Working spouses should go to their employer first before using Armstrong's P.P.O. plan.**
Remember, Armstrong is self-funded and every dollar you spend on insurance comes from the profits of Armstrong International. If we have less profit, we are not as strong financially, which prevents us from doing other programs to benefit you. Be fair. If your spouse works for another company, have your spouse use the insurance where he/she works before using Armstrong's.

4. **Prescription drugs or generic drugs**.
You will save yourself and the company money if you ask for generic drugs. If you ask your doctor to prescribe generic, she will tell you if generic is acceptable. Bill Hartman, Sr. reminds us all that our retirees, which *you* will be one day, are fortunate to participate in Armstrong's prescription plan. Many retirees cannot afford the pills their doctors prescribe so they go without. Most companies

do _not_ offer insurance coverage for retirees because prescriptions cost too much. The Armstrong retirees pay little out of their pocket to receive their medication. Just another good reason to retire from Armstrong International.

9.
IT'S YOUR FAULT

This morning on her way to work, Renee Wang from our engineering department was driving up Commodity Circle to Armstrong Service, Inc. when a car suddenly turned from the right hand lane in front of her causing an accident. Since the accident was virtually in front of our office, some of Renee's co-workers went out to check on Renee and the other people involved in the accident.

When an accident occurs, everyone wants to place the blame on someone, and in this case it was clearly the fault of the other driver, not Renee. Imagine how it would feel to cause an accident and to have the accident occur in front of the other person's place of work. The person whose car you struck is getting hugs, support, and questions of concern from their associates. Under these circumstances, I'm sure it made the people feel even worse.

Donna Sealy noticed how upset the lady and her husband both were about the accident and took the time to offer them comfort while she learned their story. They were on their way to a doctor's appointment for the husband. The next morning he was scheduled for a bone scan to confirm or rule out cancer. Donna retrieved her bible and read scripture to the upset couple, then prayed with them for a favorable diagnosis after tomorrow's appointment. She then invited the couple into Armstrong Service to offer them a cold drink to help calm them.

> *Kind words can be short and easy to speak, but their echoes are truly endless.*
> — *Mother Teresa*

The Moral Of The Story

1. **Kindness without practice make but half an artist.**
This couple will surely drive by our office many times in the future as they go to and from their doctor's appointments. When they do they will look at our building and remember the caring people like Donna Sealy who brought a little bit of comfort to them in their time of trouble. In this country it has become politically incorrect to read the bible or to pray while you are at work, school, or anywhere outside of your own home or church. I respect Donna because I know she does not do these things to draw attention to herself, or in a way that interferes with her work duties, she does it because that is who she is!

2. **Losing your temper is no way to get rid of it.**
Renee didn't become angry with the couple, even though she had support from her fellow co-workers. It would have been easy. Renee forgave them.

STORIES
TO TURN US INTO **CHANGE** GOURMETS

CHAPTER 3

10.
TIE DAY

"Why didn't somebody tell me to wear a tie today? I would have been happy to wear one. Instead, I'm wearing a sweater." I remember thinking this yesterday morning while visiting Armstrong-Yoshitake (A-Y). Let me explain why I needed to wear a tie by starting at the beginning of this story.

While visiting A-Y in Three Rivers, Michigan, I bumped into Rex Scare, Purchasing, Production & Engineering Manager. While talking to Rex, my eyes became glued to the cartoon character that was on his tie. I remember saying, "That looks like a fun tie to wear." Rex nodded with a smile. Shortly thereafter, I found myself visiting with Tim Jones and Tom Hyatt. We were talking about sales in general, when again I noticed that Tim and Tom were wearing a tie. More cartoon characters! Then it hit me. Everybody had a tie on. Even a couple of the ladies. This is very unusual, I thought to myself. The A-Y people normally dress very casually. There must be a meeting or special guest in town and they forgot to tell me. Why didn't someone warn me to wear a tie today? I walked into the General Manager's office.

"Larry, when's the meeting today? I noticed everybody has a tie on?"

"There's no meeting. Oh, I know what's got you confused. Every Monday is tie day at A-Y."

STORIES TO TURN US INTO CHANGE GOURMETS

Character day.

THE MORAL OF THE STORY

1. **Ahead of our time . . . and proud of it.**
We now have Armstrong Characters at Armstrong International. Each of these characters must talk and <u>dress</u> the part of their character. Please refer to my story, "Armstrong Characters," found in my latest book, <u>Once Told, They're Gold</u>. I believe Armstrongers should start coming to work dressed as the character they play at work. We have gone from dress up day to casual day, to now, **character** day. Sometime in the future, this will become popular, much as casual day has become popular, and once again we will be ahead of our time. Dressing as Armstrong Characters is not only fun for our employees, but memorable to our customers, our partners, and Armstrong Steam University students. If we're memorable, they will remember to buy Armstrong products.

2. **Change with the times.**
I'm not talking about thin ties being in and fat ties being out of style. I'm talking about changing the dress code of corporate America. Suits and ties and business suits for women used to be the preferred dress code at businesses throughout America. Today, these companies are changing to a more casual environment. Why? Because employees like Tom, Tim, Rex and Larry are demanding it. The new generation wants to be comfortable at work. To attract these new recruits, and keep our current employees, changing the dress code makes good business sense. "Casual" does not mean "sloppy." Tie day says it loud and

clear. A-Y has a casual dress code _every_ day except Monday, when you are required to dress up with a tie. How many companies are still out there bragging about _one_ casual day a week? Too many I suspect.

3. **David Armstrong is coming to town tomorrow so wear a tie.**
How many companies insist that their employees dress up when the boss or owner comes to town? You may have guessed, but nobody gets dressed up for me. Bravo! May we become brave enough to dress casually when customers come to town? Better yet, as Armstrong Characters.

11.

PLEASE REMEMBER ME

"Have you heard......Brian Nimtz is leaving the company?"

"No way! I just talked to him yesterday. He seemed really happy with his job."

"That's what I thought!"

"Why is he leaving? Did they fire him or is he leaving on his own?"

"He's leaving on his own. He has a new job."

Later that day a call was made to Steve Gibson, Chief Financial Officer, who was Brian's boss. Brian told Steve that he was turning in his resignation. Brian offered to work to the end of the month, which Steve accepted. Steve then came over to my office and told me the sad news. Both of us shook our heads in disbelief. Neither of us had seen this coming. What warning signals did we miss which would have alerted us that Brian was thinking about leaving? Read the morals below while thinking about your employees.

Look for changes in behavior.

THE MORAL OF THE STORY

1. **Our best employees are not looking for new jobs.** They are being actively recruited. Before the ink was dry on this story, I heard that Chris Vogel, from Armstrong Fluid

Handling was leaving. She was recruited by a friend while attending a wedding.

2. **Loss of interest in work.**
Chris had told her boss, Cam, that she wanted to travel less. **RED FLAG!** Chris was in sales. Salespeople travel. Was Chris losing interest in her job? The new job she took did change her career path.

3. **Closed door conversations.**
Neither Brian nor Chris did this, but keep an eye open for the closed doors.

4. **Takes more time off than normal.**
This is very common when an employee is interviewing. Interviews are given during company hours. Those same hours they need to report to work. Only one solution--take time off.

5. **Calls in sick more often than normal.**
I stand corrected, this is another solution.

6. **Spends less time with fellow workers.**
They may be afraid of saying something or may feel ashamed that they are leaving.

7. **Don't forget the exit interview.**
The employee who is leaving has no reason to lie. No fear of their boss. You may learn something to stop the next employee from leaving. If you're lucky you will hear good things, which is what I heard from Brian and Chris.

Story Update:

Chris Vogel lasted almost 1 year. The new career was not what she hoped it would be. Chris remembered how she enjoyed working at Armstrong and asked to come back. We happily said, **"YES!"**

12.
HEINZ

It all started on April 25, 2000, the first meeting of Heinz employees with Armstrong Service. Armstrong Service was negotiating a contract to purchase the Boiler Room and manage the steam and air systems. I, Dan Dipple, was a 13-year employee of Heinz and somewhat skeptical of how Armstrong Service would treat the boiler room employees and what was going to be offered to keep us here.

Mr. Eric Hager presented the overview to the boiler room employees and stressed Armstrong's core values. I simply couldn't believe what I was hearing. Hearing the stories from Eric made Armstrong Service sound like a fairytale. Then Mr. David Armstrong introduces himself and gives out three books that tell stories of the management style of Armstrong Service. All of this sounded too good to be true! I had to see it to believe it.

Yep! You guessed it. I went to Armstrong International in Three Rivers and saw with my own eyes! Not only does Armstrong Service have stories, they practice what they preach! The open and unattended cash box, Main Street, signing in with crayons, animal buggies, and most important .....PRIDE! Each employee from Three Rivers was proud of being a member of the Armstrong family and most had their own story to tell. I was very impressed and couldn't wait to become a member of the Armstrong Team.

And wait, I did! The expected contract signing was slated for June 1st. Then the 15th of June. Before you knew it, it was July 1st, then July 15th. A problem with the verbiage in the contract language was blamed. Eric Hager continued to update us throughout the process and asked us to be patient. August 1st was targeted as "the date", then August 15th. Finally, on September 1, 2000 Armstrong Service officially owned the boiler room equipment and air compressors. The deal was done and butterflies began flying in my stomach. Was this too good to be true? Am I making the right choice by joining Armstrong Service? Will Armstrong Service uphold their commitments to the boiler room employees?

The answers to those questions are yes, yes, and YES! To date, I have been an Armstrong Service employee for 39 days. Not only has Armstrong Service lived up to my expectations, they have exceeded them. Every person that I have met from Armstrong Service has been friendly, professional, and excited about the opportunities that surround the Muscatine Operation for Armstrong Service. We will undergo many changes and challenges here in Muscatine as well as other Armstrong Service sites. It is my belief that Armstrong Service is leading the industry in energy conservation as well as many other items. I feel very fortunate to have the opportunity to join the Armstrong Team and I, Dan Dipple, am proud to say, "I work for Armstrong Service"!

Change favors the willing mind—Louis Pasteur.

THE MORAL OF THE STORY

1. **Change is not something you fear, it's something you relish.**
Dan Dipple had been an employee of Heinz for 13 years. What this story does not tell you is that if Dan accepted the new job at Armstrong Service, he could not go back to Heinz. In other words, his choice was final. When the story ends, you realize Dan had accepted the job at Armstrong Service. Most people would think Dan to be a fool, crazy or maybe that he hated working at Heinz. Not true! I'm proud to say we have one more Armstronger by the name of Dan Dipple who relishes change.

STORIES
ABOUT HAVING **FUN**

CHAPTER 4

13.

ARMSTRONG'S FIRE DEPARTMENT

Believe it or not, Armstrong International has its own fire department. This department is large enough that we have our own fire chief and many volunteer firemen. One important thing was missing in this department besides the spotted dog. You guessed it — a fire truck! Armstrong-Yoshitake is about to fix that problem.

Armstrong-Yoshitake had purchased a used delivery truck. The motor was in good shape, but the body was falling apart with a lot of rust and holes in the side panels. Don English and Mike Wolfe decided to pull off the panels and rebuild the truck. Don and Mike wanted to build a fire truck. They ordered large sheets of stainless steel, which they bent into doors, panels and the cab. Once assembled, they painted it bright fire engine red. Don had been given an aluminum ladder from the city's fire department, which was damaged. He cut a small piece from the ladder and attached it to the side of the new fire truck. An old piece of fire hose was neatly coiled in the truck. They even attached some red and white emergency lights to the cab. Don and Mike hope to find a siren which we've all heard as fire trucks race to a fire. Now the only thing missing is the spotted dog.

> *They laughed at Joan of Arc, but she went right ahead and built it anyway.* — Gracie Allen

THE MORAL OF THE STORY

1. **Few things cost so little and buy so many smiles.**
Everybody talks about physical fitness. What about mental fitness? Improve the morale of your people. Get them to chuckle.

2. **Follow the spilled water to find the fun.**
Don and Mike will use their fire truck to transport products between Armstrong-Yoshitake and Armstrong International. Three city blocks separate the two companies. This fire truck will be faster than using fork trucks. Not only will this fire truck get people to laugh, but it will improve efficiency as well. Money well spent.

3. **People rarely succeed at anything unless they have fun doing it.**
Why is that? Armstrongers often do a better job servicing the customer if they have fun. Armstrongers build better quality if work is fun. Armstrongers create new, exciting products when they have fun. Armstrongers work better together when having fun. Armstrongers never need to leave to find a job that is more fun. Don and Mike understand the value of fun.

4. **Armstrong characters . . .**
Don and Mike just became Armstrong characters — firemen. They even made their own prop — a fire truck.

Now all they need is a toy stuffed animal — you know which one. It has black spots.

14.

A PIECE OF FUN

Come with me to 221 Armstrong Boulevard. Each and every day an Armstronger from Armstrong Fluid Handling, Armstrong-Yoshitake, and Armstrong-Lynnwood can be found in the lunchroom hunting for goodies to eat. In the lunchroom stands a table. Gathered around this table were Armstrongers working on a project during lunch break. They were having lots of fun and smiling. One day I overheard these Armstrongers,

"There, it's finished."
"So that's what it looks like."
"Wow, let's do it again!"
"Yeah, this was a good idea."

Several days earlier, Kathy Duncan, Inside Order Entry for Armstrong-Yoshitake, found herself at a garage sale. As she rummaged through the items for sale, something caught her eye.

"I wonder if we could use this at Armstrong-Yoshitake," she thought. "Wouldn't it be fun?"
She picked up the puzzle box. Twenty-five cents was the price. Kathy bought it, and that's the rest of the story.

Fun is contagious.

THE MORAL OF THE STORY

1. **A disease worth catching**.
Kathy's got it. She's caught that fun bug. We find Kathy wanting to have fun at work. She also wants to help her fellow Armstrongers have fun. You can't imagine the pride I felt when I heard that Kathy bought this puzzle on the weekend. Holy smokes, she was still thinking about work on the weekend!

2. **The cure for the common boring job** . . . does not have to be expensive.
You will notice in the story that Kathy only paid 25 cents for the puzzle. A small investment to bring fun to the people at Armstrong-Yoshitake, Armstrong Fluid Handling and Armstrong-Lynnwood.

3. **Fun, funner, funnest.**
You may not know this, but we have checkerboards on lunch tables for people to play with. Another good example of having fun inexpensively. Kathy's idea was one better than my checkerboards. You see, with checkers, only two people can play. With a puzzle, more than two can have fun together.

4. **Having fun is the quickest way to make friends and keep friends**.
We have hired a lot of new Armstrongers in the past year. I can't think of a quicker way for them to become friends with the people they work with than by putting a puzzle together. Friendship is very important if you plan to work with somebody for a lifetime!

15.

NICOLE'S CRAYONS

Just the other day, I found Nicole Mason, Tim Jones' daughter, painting in the Armstrong parking lot. I walked over to her.

"What are you painting Nicole?"

"Crayons."

"Oh, you're right, it is a crayon, I can even see the wrapper on the crayon. You've done a nice job."

"Thank you. I am going to use different colors as I paint each crayon. The only area that was difficult was painting the word crayon."

"Where did you get the idea to paint crayons?"

"Sandy Conroy and I came up with the idea after Rex Scare and my dad asked for ideas on ways to make our parking lot special."

"Well, it looks fantastic Nicole, be careful not to get hit by any cars."

Later that day, I found Rex and Tim in the lobby. "I like the idea of painting crayons in the parking lot."

Tim smiled, "We thought Sandy and Nicole had a good idea. It will match the lobby where we have our guest's sign in with crayons." Refer to my story "Crayola® Crayons" in my book <u>Once Told, They're Gold.</u>

"How's that for having fun here at Armstrong-Yoshitake?" asked Rex.

® Crayola is a registered trademark of Binney & Smith

> *Imagine working for a company when you can't wait for vacation to end.*

THE MORAL OF THE STORY

1. **Believe none of what you hear and half of what you see.**
If you were applying for a job at Armstrong, seeing our parking lot with painted crayons instead of boring white parking space lines, may convince you to accept a job with Armstrong. Everybody talks a good game — remember, believe none of what you hear and half of what you see.

2. **On-the-job-fun.**
We all believe in on-the-job-training. Why not on-the-job-fun?

3. **"He who does not look ahead remains behind." —A Spanish Proverb.**
A parking lot is more than a place to park cars. It's a billboard for our company. It speaks louder and clearer than any policy manual. In the future, I see parking lots as one of a company's most valuable assets — an opportunity to sell company culture. Nicole's crayons shows Armstrong International is fun to work for.

4. **"Too many people grow up. That's the real trouble with the world, too many people grow up."– Walt Disney.**
Look at the empire Walt Disney built — and it's all based on having fun. Who would have thought you could entertain children and adults with animated movies. How about

building a theme park called Disney World with live Disney characters. How many of us wish we could work at Disney? Most of us—right? That's the point. Have fun and keep your employees from leaving.

16.

LOOK...IT'S THE BLIMP

Have you ever had the experience of flying in the Goodyear Blimp? Armstrong International has a blimp which is piloted by Jim Daugherty. One day, while behind the controls, Jim was completing his flight plan.

"We are heading southwest. We will continue that course for three more minutes and then turn south. I have a slight headwind of about 10 miles per hour. My ETA should be 7 minutes."

Slowly, the Armstrong blimp changes its course to south, drops to an altitude of 10 feet, and just clears the doorway of General Manager, Tom Grubka. Tom is on the phone as the blimp floats into his office. When he sees the blimp, he shakes his head and smiles.

Several weeks earlier, Armstrong lab technician, Bill Horton, was on an airplane returning home. In the seat in front of him he noticed a magazine that advertised a radio-controlled blimp. He thought this would be the perfect prop for the Armstrong Stadium.

When he returned to work he asked his manager, Jim Daugherty, "Jim, can we buy this blimp?"

"If I can be the pilot," responded Jim.

They immediately made the purchase. Before they flew it in Armstrong Stadium, they decided to take it for a test flight with the destination being the General Manager's office.

Several years earlier, David Armstrong was talking to a group of college students in Armstrong Stadium. David was trying to get these college students to be more creative so he asked, "You are now sitting in a conference room that looks like a baseball stadium. Look at all the creativity in here. What could we add to make our stadium more realistic?" Only one hand came up and the young lady said, "Where's the blimp?"

> Make your own magic.
> — Walt Disney

THE MORAL OF THE STORY

1. **Imagination is the highest kite you can fly...or should I say blimp**.
Bill Horton may be a lab technician, but he has the imagination of a child. Bill was thinking about how to make Armstrong a more fun place to work—even while on vacation.

2. **"Once you get people laughing, they are listening, and you can tell them almost anything"—Herb Gardner.**
It is always a challenge to hold a meeting and get everyone to listen. Our blimp gets people to laugh, thus listen. If I had a message to remember after the meeting, I would have the words light up on the blimp. Why? It would be fun to read, thus more memorable.

3. **The new Armstronger.**
In the past, employees worked for one company most of their careers and at the end of their thirty years, they would receive a gold watch. No longer! Today, employee turnover is higher. Employees are not afraid to switch companies. Money is a motivator, but so is a job full of challenge, opportunity to advance in management and better benefits. Armstrong International will also use fun, I mean **FUN**, to keep employees positively energized!

17.
BE KIND TO ANIMALS

Willard Vedmore almost always locks his car in the Armstrong parking lot. It's his way of reducing the risk of paybacks for his own pranks against fellow Armstrong employees. However, he did forget to lock his truck one day this April.

On that fateful day, the stars were aligned, spring was in the air and Richard Wright was in the yard when he saw the squirrel forget to look both ways before crossing the street. Rich went to the road to check on the little guy, but he had gone to gather nuts in squirrel heaven. It was quick. There were no marks, no blood, but his work on this earth was clearly over. That was until Rich showed the dead animal to David Casterline and he noted that Willard's truck was unlocked. The squirrel had one more role to play.

They propped the departed squirrel in the passenger seat and cleverly rolled the passenger side window down part way to make it appear the little varmint had found his way into the car by himself.

David waited out of sight by the back door when Willard left at the end of the day. Fate had arranged another surprise in the form of Ken Handy who had asked Willard for a ride home that day.

Ken shouted, "There's a squirrel in there!" He retreated leaving the door open.

"He must have come in through the window", yelled Willie as he fell back to a safe distance.

The commotion went on for some time until ex-Marine, James Bucholtz came to their rescue and determined the animal's state of health and removed it from the truck. About that time Willard noticed David in hysterics inside the office door and realized he'd been the target of a prank. We all have come to realize that Willard is still way ahead of us. We have all fallen victim to his pranks and put down by his off-the-cuff remarks. We will never catch up, but a little retaliation is sweet.

Ye shall be known by your alumni. – Tom Peters

THE MORAL OF THE STORY

1. **Ye shall be known by your alumni.**
Who do you hang out with? Are they entrepreneur's, self-starters, are they funny, or are they serious. One can learn a great deal about somebody if you watch whom they hang with. I know James and David to be pranksters because they hang out with Willie. Ken and Rich may act serious but they also like to play jokes on fellow Armstrongers. So, how would you work with or lead Ken, Rich, David, James and Willie?

2. **Having fun is the quickest way to make friends with co-workers.**
Almost everybody likes Willie. I've never had a complaint about Willie. As a leader I like that because I have enough employee problems throughout the day.

3. **Do you have a Court Jester in your company?**
I always wanted to hire a comedian for Armstrong. Think of all the fun I would have in the interviews. A Court Jester would also make Armstrong an enjoyable place to work. If you are interested, don't bother applying for the job it's already taken by Willie Vedmore. Now, it's time to change Willie's title on his business cards to Court Jester. Remember to make a promotion very special because employees receive very few in a lifetime. Yes, this is a promotion. Really — I'm serious!

18.

COURT JESTER

This mysterious object was difficult to identify. There it was, and there was no denying it. Its bright colors of red, purple, yellow, and orange brought it to life. The three little balls seemed to dance in the air. There was shape to it, yet, it had no shape. It seemed to go in all directions, like it had a mind of its own. It was the perfect hat for Armstrong's Court Jester, Willie Vedmore. You've seen these hats in books, or maybe in a circus, or at the Las Vegas Cirque du Soleil show. Actually, that's where I purchased the hat, knowing it was the perfect costume for Willie Vedmore who had just been promoted to Armstrong Court Jester. I presented the hat to Willie in front of his apprentice James Bucholtz, who was over 20 years younger and looked forward to the day that he could become Court Jester.

I gave the Court Jester hat to Willie and said, "You know Willie, this is part of your costume as Armstrong's Court Jester. You've got the business card that says Court Jester, and now you have the hat."

"Thanks Dave, I really like it!" Willie placed it on his head.

"No Willie, you've got it on backwards. I want to make sure that you put it on right, because you have to wear it around the company."

"This is perfect timing. I have a meeting in fifteen minutes, I'll wear it there."

STORIES ABOUT HAVING FUN   55

"I was hoping you would say something like that Willie. If not, I was going to take away your title and give it to James. You have to be willing to dress the part and act the part if you want the title of Court Jester."

Later that day, I found Willie in his office. "How'd it go, Willie, with the hat at the meeting?"

"David, they loved it. It was a pretty serious meeting about production control, but when I wore the hat, it broke the tension in the meeting. I told a couple of jokes, and after that, things went pretty smooth."

"Outstanding, Willie. I knew I didn't make a mistake when I promoted you to Court Jester."

Proud as a peacock.

THE MORAL OF THE STORY

1. **All things are difficult before they are easy.**
I remember the first time I asked Jan Blasius to dress up as a ballpark vendor for Armstrong Stadium. Asking her to wear a red and white striped outfit, sunglasses, and a tray around her neck filled with bags of popcorn and soda while in Armstrong Stadium was not easy. Jan did it and had a good time. More Armstrong characters soon followed. A few years later, in front of 300 people, I made an announcement where I promoted Willard Vedmore, who was Production Manager, and added a second title, Court Jester. It was difficult standing in front of my peers and promoting something that they might consider foolish. Then I remembered Jan's laugh as she wore her costume. It gave me strength.

2. **All things are easier when done willingly**.

It was easy promoting Willie to Court Jester, because he was willing. If he wasn't willing, there were two other individuals, James Bucholtz and Matt Tisch, who were hoping to get the title.

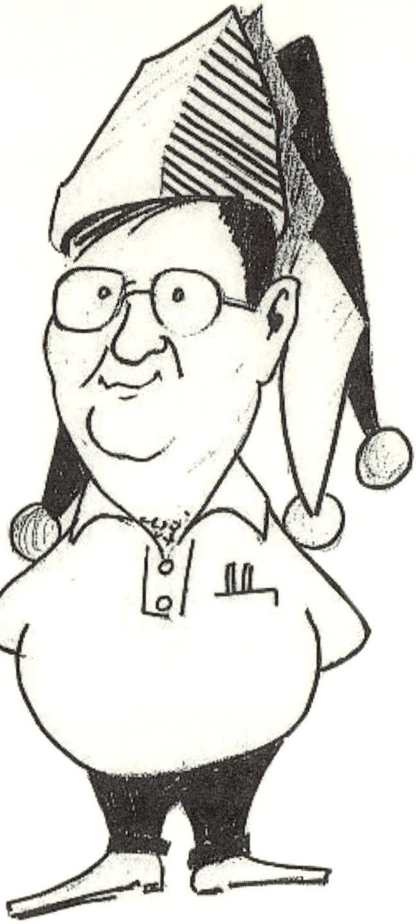

19.
LET'S MAKE AN ARMSTRONG DEAL

"Welcome to **Let's Make An Armstrong Deal**," announces the game host. There, in front of the contestants, hang three curtains. The rules are simple; choose one curtain and the prize behind it is yours. The prizes are Armstrong products ranging from several thousand dollars to a few dollars. The game host selects a customer wearing an Armstrong hat.

"Which curtain would you like?"

"I'll take, uh, curtain number two", answers the contestant.

"Before we show you what's behind curtain number two, let's see what's behind curtain number one." The curtain goes up and there sits a pumping trap valued at $2,000.

The contestant sighs in disappointment.

"That's OK. There could still be a good prize behind curtain number two."

"I hope so. I am really hoping it's a water heater because we need one in our company."

"Well, how sure are you that it's behind your curtain? What if I were to give you a 5% discount?" The game host pulls out a wad of Armstrong discount dollar bills and places 5% in his hand. "Do you still want curtain number two?"

"Yes."

STORIES ABOUT HAVING FUN

"What if I gave you 10%, 15%?"

"Oh boy, 15% off my next purchase? No, I am going to stick with curtain number two."

"Well, let me show you what you would have won if you had chosen curtain number three." The curtain goes up and there behind it is an Armstrong-Lynnwood yellow steam hose. Value — $360.00. Everybody sighs.

"So, you're still feeling pretty good about your choice?"

"Yes, sir. I just know it's a water heater."

"How sure are you? What if I gave you 20% off your next purchase?" The host places another 5% discount in the contestant's hand.

"I still want the curtain."

"Here's my final offer — 25%."

In the audience you can hear his fellow classmates yell, "Take the discount! Take the discount! No, take the curtain!"

"What will it be?" asks the game host.

"The curtain! I'll take the curtain!"

He gives the discount money back to the game host.

"Well let's see what's behind curtain number two."

The curtain slowly lifts and there behind it is an Armstrong GP2000K1 Pressure Reducing Valve. Value — $800.00. The contestant smiles with a sigh of relief and the audience cheers while the game host says, "Thank you for playing **Let's Make An Armstrong Deal.**"

No costumes required.

THE MORAL OF THE STORY

1. **Who was the contestant?**
He was a guest who was attending Armstrong Steam University (ASU). This guest, who was an Armstrong customer, was on a campus tour with the rest of his classmates when we staged our show—**Let's Make An Armstrong Deal**.

2. **Who was the game host?**
He was yours truly. Our main purpose is to have fun with **Let's Make An Armstrong Deal**, but also to offer a possible prize, an Armstrong product, to one of our customers. When they take their prize back to their company, they will be a hero. They will also be using an Armstrong product and we hope this will encourage them to purchase more Armstrong products in the future.

3. **Even if we lose, we win.**
If the customer picks the right curtain and wins an expensive product, we still win because they will be using an Armstrong product. Remember, these are mostly Armstrong customers who come to ASU. If they are not a customer already, maybe having fun at Armstrong is all it takes to convert them into buying Armstrong products.

4. **I'll take the discount!**
What we decided to do was offer an extra discount on the next purchase of <u>one</u> item only. We printed up some Armstrong fun money in increments of 5%. This gave the

game host a chance to lay 5% discount money in the hands of the customer. If they still chose the curtain, they had to return the discount paper money. If they kept the discount, a General Manager must sign the discount bills where it says "Treasurer." The reason for this was to protect ourselves from the loss of any discount bills that we kept in storage. They were only valid if signed by a General Manager. Which General Manager? The one who had a product behind the curtain the customer chose before taking the discount.

5. **The curtains.**
The curtains were actually overhead doors in the shipping department which were used to load trucks. It was the perfect location at the end of a tour, and there was plenty of space for thirty customers, or should we call them the audience, to sit back and watch as **Let's Make An Armstrong Deal** was played with one of their fellow classmates. We had the artist, Paddy Aiden, paint the numbers one, two and three on the doors. Painted curtains were added too.

6. **Applause, Applause, Applause!**
Don't forget to set the mood. Have pre-recorded applauses or sighs of disbelief or laughter and play it at appropriate times throughout **Let's Make An Armstrong Deal**. We also put Armstrongers in the audience and had them lead the audience by cheering and clapping. If you can't afford to pre-record, then make some cardboard signs and write applause and laughter on them and hold them up at appropriate times. Remember, we want to get the audience

involved. They too are customers. The game should not be fun for just one, but for all!

STORIES
TO GET PEOPLE TO **COMMUNICATE** ABOUT THINGS WORTH **COMMUNICATING** ABOUT

CHAPTER 5

20.

THE PROBLEM WITH PLANT TOURS

You are about to hear a tragic story. The tragedy is that you and I are the characters in this story, or should I say "victims." Most of us, at one time or another, have been on a plant tour. This tour may have been at your own company or while visiting someone else's company. All of these tours have had one thing in common. You <u>can't</u> hear what the guide is saying. This is especially true when the groups are large. Only the first few people in the front of the group can hear. The machinery is loud, the guide is speaking softly, someone in the group is talking at the same time, or other noises drown out what the guide is saying. What a waste of time! The only person receiving benefit from the tour is the guide, who is able to brag about his company. I have even seen this kind of tour at Armstrong International. Not too long ago, to solve this problem, we came up with the idea of having the guide use a megaphone while talking. This idea was good, but we came up with an even better idea. You know those headsets that you see diplomats wearing in the United Nations? They are normally used to translate what is being said in all of the different languages. Why not use these headsets for shop tours? We bought 40 sets. The guides speak into a wireless microphone which transmits his words to these headsets. The headsets also block out the plant noise. It works great, and there are other benefits, too. Read the morals to find them.

> *If you take the time to give a tour, make sure they can hear you.*

THE MORAL OF THE STORY

1. **Use these headsets in your seminars.**
Armstrong International gives technical product seminars on steam, air, hydronics and saving energy. The classes are normally large, about 30 people — and most of the time, everything can be heard. During seminars for our <u>foreign</u> visitors, it is more difficult for the seminar instructor to be heard because a lot of translating is going on in the audience. Some guests speak more English than others and help their colleagues by translating. We hired a translator to interpret what the speaker said so that each person could hear it in their own language. She spoke into the microphone so all would hear through their headsets. This kept our seminars quiet and made it easier for everyone to hear and <u>understand</u>.

2. **We use our headsets while giving seminars on the road**.
When we were giving a seminar in our manufacturing company in Beijing, China, we knew the speaker would be English speaking and would need to be translated into Chinese. Again, this would cause confusion. Therefore, we took the headsets with us to China. Why should they be used in only one location? Armstrongers take their laptop computers on the road, so why not headsets?

3. **People will listen to you if they can hear you**.
When giving a speech, seminar, plant tour or presentation in a meeting, remember that if they can't hear you they

can't learn from you. So speak up. Look for those hearing aides, people in the back of a large group, or those whom you know don't hear well.

21.

DO YOU SPEAK ENGLISH?

I remember once being halfway around the world in the country of Thailand. While hearing Larry Daugherty give a presentation on Armstrong's Flo-Rite Temp® water-heater to our sales representative (Alpha Group Company Ltd.), I was asked to visit with the Managing Director. Mr. Somboon had a large notebook on a conference table. When I sat down, he handed me a fax from Armstrong Machine Works. The fax notified Alpha Group Company of a partial shipment, and this concerned Mr. Somboon. He then slid a piece of paper across the table to me. It was their purchase order, and on the purchase order he pointed to shipping instructions. It said 'no partial shipment'. As I re-read the Armstrong fax, it was obvious that some of the product had already been shipped. I re-read the fax several times even though the handwriting was clear, to make sure I understood the message correctly. I did. It was Armstrong's mistake. I agreed to solve the problem by paying the additional freight and extra duties due for the partial shipment, but then I asked a more important question.

"Mr. Somboon, do you always receive answers to your faxes in handwriting?"

"Oh yes, it is very common." He opened the large notebook and revealed several past faxes all in handwriting. "This is a problem for us, for many times we cannot read the handwriting because it's too sloppy. You don't even use a reference number. Your people just write an answer on our fax and send it back."

I reviewed each fax and could tell that some were very difficult to read. Not everyone's handwriting was clear.

While flying home, I had 26 hours to write this story. I have witnessed this kind of poor communication many times in the past. The following morals will establish a new policy for all Armstrong International divisions when communicating with other countries.

Justifying a fault doubles it.

THE MORAL OF THE STORY

1. **Everybody speaks English.**
It's true! All the business people in all of countries that I have visited have spoken English and have wanted to practice speaking English when I was there. We Americans, except for a few, are too lazy to learn another language. We always justify this by saying that since everybody speaks English, why should we learn another language? The first thing we must do is change our attitude, not toward learning a new language, but on ways to improve the way we communicate in our native tongue—English.

2. **You learned a foreign language while in grade school**.
Let me refresh your memory. The words you used were two syllables, not three or four. You wrote in short sentences; you used very few adjectives and adverbs; you wrote big...I'm sorry, you probably did not write until sixth grade, you printed. Practice your **grade** school English when you

respond to our sales force and customers overseas. Be careful <u>not</u> to use past or future tenses. I try to use the present tense whenever possible. If you've ever taken a foreign language you understand how difficult tenses are. Proper grammar is not as important as clear communication.

3. **Speak slowly.**
I can't tell you how many times I have listened to Armstrongers speaking quickly when the other person is trying to translate. How rude and ignorant. Speak slowly and repeat yourself as often as possible. Also, try to use the same words repeatedly no matter how childish it sounds. Remember, your goal is to communicate clearly.

22.

TARGET PRACTICE

"Bullseye!!!" yells a guest.

"Nice shot!! Now I want you to shoot the Armstrong Inverted Bucket Steam Trap."

The customer carefully aims the gun from the Armstrong-Lynnwood Hose Station at the target. Pssssssssssshhhh goes the gun as a stream of hot water hits its intended target 30 feet away.

"Congratulations. You're in first place at this moment," announces Paul Knight, Vice President of Armstrong-Lynnwood, Inc. "Step over to the side and let's give another seminar attendee a chance to match your record."

A big Texan walks up. "Let me have that gun. I'll show you how to shoot."

Paul hands him the gun and says, "I want you to find the Armstrong Pump Trap and shoot the target on it."

"Which one is that?" he asks.

"I can't tell you, that's part of the contest. You've been in our seminars all week and we've identified our products."

He takes careful aim and Pssssssssssshhh, hot water flies across the air missing its target. His hands tighten down on the gun as he pulls the trigger a second time —pssssssssshh.

"Nice shot!" comments Paul.

Fifteen minutes later:

Only one guest had hit all <u>her</u> targets and properly identified them. Paul took her down to the Armstrong General Store where she was allowed to pick out anything of her liking as a prize for her shooting skill and steam knowledge.

Shooting an Armstrong–Lynnwood's hose gun is more convincing than any spoken word or penned thought.

THE MORAL OF THE STORY

1. **"Curiosity and fun are handmaidens." — Tom Peters, business author.**
During our educational seminars, I am sure our guests (customers) are curious about how easy it is to aim the gun for the Armstrong–Lynnwood hose station. We may have taught our guests everything there is to know about the hose station, but actually pulling the trigger and watching the hot water hit its target provided a fun experience which will help them remember the product better than a thousand words could ever communicate.

2. **Know your target before you shoot it.**
Each Armstrong Steam University class provides technical steam knowledge and identification of Armstrong products. Armstrong–Lynnwood introduces their products at the end of the seminars. Therefore, all Armstrong products have been identified before Paul Knight takes them out to shoot at the targets. Paul has each customer identify the product before shooting it. If they shoot the wrong product, it

counts as a miss. We find out very quickly if our classes are successful at identifying Armstrong products for the customers. This is better than any questionnaire filled out at the end of a seminar.

23.

VOICE MAIL

It all started with, "I'm sorry, I am not in the office right now. Please leave a message after the tone and I will return your call." The real tragedy in this story was that I had heard the same message six times in a row while trying to find a live body to talk to! Now, I must admit that a few times I pushed the "0" on the phone pad to get the switchboard. At this point I would get a live operator and she would transfer me to the next person. Unfortunately, each time I was transferred, I heard the message "I'm sorry, I am not in the office right now. Please leave a message after the tone and I will return your call."

A few days later I found myself in Belgium preparing to celebrate the 30th anniversary of Armstrong International, S.A. Ron Schlesch had been in Belgium for a few days and had tried to make calls to Armstrong in Michigan. Ron told me that all he was getting was voice mail; he couldn't get anybody to answer the phone. Roger Clossett overheard our conversation and added, "Me too!"

Voice mail does not kill; it permits suicide.

THE MORAL OF THE STORY

1. **Suicide?**
Many Armstrongers will use voice mail to avoid being interrupted while working on a project, taking a break, when it's close to lunch or quitting time, or simply not answering a neighbor's phone. Voice mail can be good if used properly. Refer to my story, "Three Telephone Rings" in my book Once Told, They're Gold.

2. **A company is known by the way it answers its phone.**
Keep the human touch alive for our customer's, make them feel unique and special. Today, getting a live person is special. You think you've won the lotto. A live voice says "we care"; "we want to treat you like a person'", "you are important". After all, most of us prefer working with people, not machines.

3. **A live voice is mightier than the pen, e-mail or voice mail.**
The human voice builds personal relationships. A live Armstronger draws more knowledge from a customer phone call than voice mail does. No questions can be asked, no explanation given, no clarification about what was said is possible with voice mail. People sell service, products, image, comfort, peace of mind, and confidence, not voice mail.

24.

I FOUND A MESSAGE IN A BOTTLE

The bottle was in good shape. Inside was a rolled up piece of red paper. I could hardly wait to open the bottle and read it. What hidden treasure had I found? I popped the cap and carefully pulled out the message. I unrolled it slowly and began to read.

A few weeks earlier...

I flew to Muscatine, Iowa to visit a Heinz plant. I was greeted by Dan Poland, General Manager of Heinz, and Eric Hager, Manager of Operation and Maintenance for Armstrong Service. Armstrong Service was in final negotiations to purchase the assets of the Heinz boiler plant. Armstrong Service had a contract with Heinz to manage their energy costs and run the boiler room, plus provide compressed air for the next 16 years. Armstrong Service received its profits by reducing the energy costs, which we shared with Heinz. My mission was to convince four Heinz employees to quit Heinz and join Armstrong Service. This would not be easy because they would still remain in Muscatine, Iowa working in the boiler plant of Heinz. We needed these Heinz employees because they had firsthand knowledge of where improvements could be made on the equipment. To ensure success, Heinz leaders were in full agreement to have Armstrong Service hire these employees.

Sunday night before my trip...

Yvonne (my wife) and I were driving home from a restaurant. I had been thinking all week about how I could motivate the Heinz employees to join Armstrong Service. The key was to be creative and to focus on improving communication. Suddenly ahead I saw my opportunity. I quickly pulled the car into the parking lot in front of Winn Dixie grocery store. "Yvonne, I need your help. Come inside with me and help me find what I am looking for." Up and down the isles we went and finally Yvonne found what I was looking for--Heinz ketchup bottles. We purchased four bottles and drove home. Once in the kitchen I began to empty their precious cargo called ketchup, into a different container. Now, I had four bottles to give the Heinz employees so they could send their messages to me.

Is a tomato a fruit? Let's talk!

THE MORAL OF THE STORY

1. **Packaging is a lost opportunity.**
Why does packaging only have to be used to hold a product? Why can't it be used for communication? I needed a way to convince the people at Heinz that they could communicate with the leaders at Armstrong International. Now remember, we were over 1,000 miles apart and the odds of them seeing me again in the near future were very slim. How was I going to build their trust and desire to communicate with me? The best way I thought was to peak their interest and curiosity. Will David get the bottle with my message?

2. **I found a message in a bottle.**
During the first two weeks after handing out the Heinz Ketchup bottles, I received two bottles with messages in them. It worked! Two of the four Heinz employees joined Armstrong Service. Guess which two?

25.

SLAM

Just the other day a tremendous bang echoed through my ear as someone slammed the phone down onto its cradle. It happened after our conversation had ended. My immediate thought was "how rude". Then I thought maybe this person couldn't wait to hang up because they didn't want to talk to me. This told me that there is an Armstrong employee that doesn't want to talk to the Chief Storytelling Officer (for those of you who are more traditional, Chief Operating Officer) of their company. If they're foolish enough to do it to me, they'd do it to everyone. You who slammed the phone down on me--read the morals to this story to improve your telephone skills. You know who you are.

Old habits are hard to break.

THE MORAL OF THE STORY

1. **Pause...** before hanging up the phone.
I always wait one second before I begin to hang up my phone. This gives the other person time to hang up before I do.

2. **Be Gentle.**
Don't <u>slam</u> the phone into the cradle. Very gently place the phone down. That way if you did not pause long enough, the person you talked to will not be insulted when they hear you hang up the phone. Hearing a phone slam down is like shouting at a person.

3. **The phone is the blood of a company.**
Remember my story "Three Telephone Rings" in my book <u>Once Told, They're Gold</u>; or my story "HELLO!" found in my book titled <u>How To Turn Your Company's Parables Into Profit</u>. I have written many stories about how to answer and handle the telephone. Simply put, just as blood keeps you and I alive, the telephone keeps a company alive.

4. **Ouch!**
My ear hurts from having the phone slammed. I know who you are!!!!

26.

MAN'S BEST FRIEND

"Hello, this is Dr. Smith, the veterinarian for Mischa, and this message is for Mischa. The pathology report came back on Mischa and confirms what I suspected. We do have a hormonal imbalance. The pathologist has ruled out all the other skin diseases. It points towards the abnormality of the sex hormones and we will be doing our blood tests next month to confirm this. Have your parents practice catching a urine sample by walking around with a small cup and bending down and catching the sample—do a lot of practice runs, because the day of your next visit I would like to have another urine sample. The sample that we looked at during your first visit was a very small sample, but it showed a lot of protein. I just want to make sure that there are no other problems going on in your urinary tract, which could spell other worries for us. Come in for your next visit with an empty stomach, and have your parents catch a urine sample. If you have any questions, call me back."

Ignorance of good communication is no excuse.

THE MORAL OF THE STORY

1. **"This message is for Mischa".**
Dr. Smith had the guts to admit that just doing all right isn't good enough. Most doctors, veterinarians, dentists, etc. have their receptionists call to schedule the next appointment. Not true with Dr. Smith. He personally called. This is very uncommon and as I have said before, the uncommon gets noticed no matter how small.

2. **A doctor's actions may save the patient, but his words show his compassion.**
Dr. Smith knew his medicine. The actions he took helped Mischa. This gave us peace of mind and hope that Mischa would be okay, but the words he used in his message showed that he cared. Notice that he talked to Mischa as if our dog were human. Don't believe me? Read the story again and look for the words: "have your parents," "during your first visit," "empty stomach," and finally, "call me back."

3. **The secret of genius is to carry the spirit of a child to work.**
Dr. Smith is an educated man. To call Mischa and leave a message for a dog, not the owner, is something a child would do. The bad news could have been a bolt from the blue, but instead, my wife couldn't wait to find me so I could listen to his phone recording. Dr. Smith had treated Mischa as if she was our child, which touched my wife's heart.

4. **We will get paid what we are worth once we prove our worth.**
Dr. Smith is a dermatologist for dogs. Yes, <u>dogs</u> not people! He is expensive, but we <u>happily</u> paid the bill because he took bad news and shared it with us so we would be teased into a smile, a laugh, or a chuckle as we heard his message to Mischa. Customers for life!

27.

THEY'RE GREAT!!! ®

The tardy bell rings and the students of the Martin County High School Leadership Class take their seat. The teacher, Mr. Dawson, assigns the project of the day. The students are to write a thank you letter to the guest speaker they heard earlier that week. The students wrote the following thank you letter:

> "Dear Mr. Armstrong:
>
> We greatly appreciated you taking time out of your day to speak to our class. Your technique of storytelling was a unique form of leadership but also very interesting. We enjoyed the story about a message found in a Heinz Ketchup bottle. We learned a lot and will always remember to have fun and be creative communicators.
>
> Sincerely,
> Mr. Dawson's Leadership Class"

When the letter was finished, they rolled it up, tied a gold string around it, and carefully placed it into a large box. "Martin County High School" was printed on the box, along with several paw prints from a tiger. Later that day the box was delivered to Armstrong International, in Stuart, Florida to the attention of David Armstrong.

When I returned from lunch, the box was waiting for me with my other mail. I quickly glanced at the box and recognized it immediately. It was a box of Kellogg's Frosted Flakes®. I picked it up and noticed it was very light. Nothing was inside; or was there? I opened the box and found the note you just read inside. I took the note out, untied the string, and read the thank you letter from the students.

THEY'RE GR-R-REAT! ® -Tony The Tiger™, Kellogg's Character.

THE MORAL OF THE STORY

1. **"I Found A Message In A Bottle".**
Do you remember this story found on page 78? Mr. Dawson's leadership class does. If you recall, I used a Heinz Ketchup bottle as an envelope for the new employees at Heinz. They put a message in the ketchup bottle for me to read. Since a tiger is the mascot for Martin County High School, it seemed natural to use Kellogg's Frosted Flakes® with Tony the Tiger™ on it. Surely I would open the empty box when I received it in the mail. But it wasn't empty, was it? A+ for the students in Mr. Dawson's leadership class!

® "They're Gr-r-reat and Kellogg's Frosted Flakes is a Registered trademark of the Kellogg's Company.

STORIES TO GET PEOPLE TO COMMUNICATE

STORIES ABOUT CORE VALUES

28.

A BORN AGAIN CHRISTIAN

Warren Wilson recalls this story: "Late one evening I heard a knock at my door. When I opened the door Miss Tompkins from hospitality was standing there. Next to her was a huge basket of flowers. I read the card and found that the flowers were from my friends at Armstrong–Yoshitake. Imagine my surprise and honor. Miss Tompkins is a very good friend of mine in charge of the dining room where I eat. I told Miss Tompkins the flowers were sent by my friends at Armstrong–Yoshitake for my 88th birthday, which is tomorrow."

"I remember my 78th birthday. I was sitting in a restaurant called 'The Seasons' with Larry Daugherty, Tom Grubka, and Cam Spence. We were making a toast to the successful completion of the Flo-Rite-Temp® lab test which led to a signed contract. We toasted the successful lab test and even though it was December they toasted my birthday."

"I am an Armstrong–Yoshitake convert. I want to call you all friends because I have never met a group of people so dedicated to proving that giving is better than receiving. I have become a Christian in my old age."

The end.
—*Warren Wilson, Inventor of Flo-Rite-Temp®*

THE MORAL OF THE STORY

1. **Happy 88th Birthday Warren.**
I remember Warren when we first met. He was a young man of 78 years. Warren had developed and held the patent rights to a water heater which he called the Flo-Rite-Temp®. Warren was looking for a company to purchase his patent rights and provide him with royalty checks. Warren had just ended a bad relationship with his previous employer and was a little unsure of Armstrong International. Could we be just like his past employer?

2. **Warren was not a greedy man.**
Armstrong-Yoshitake bought his current inventory and the patent rights. A royalty check was to be paid at 3% until the end of the patent in the year 2004. When sales hit $3,000,000 per year his 3% royalty will adjust downward on all sales over $3,000,000. Warren started this relationship with a fair price and Armstrong-Yoshitake will finish it by being more than fair with Warren. The contract only dealt with the Flo-Rite-Temp® Water Heater that Warren designed. Armstrong has made several major improvements to his design. Armstrong has created new generations of water heaters that would get around Warren's patent. Most companies are dedicated to finding ways to stop paying royalties, but not Armstrong-Yoshitake. It stands firm in its core value of fairness and loyalty. Warren was not greedy and Armstrong-Yoshitake will not become greedy.

3. **Man shall not live by bread alone. -- Matthew 4:4.**
Jesus wanted us to understand that we could not live by food alone, but also needed to live by God's word. Warren

Wilson cannot live by royalty checks alone. A kind word, a visit by the Armstrong–Yoshitake people, or a flower arrangement is needed.

4. **If you do not stand firm in your faith, you will not stand at all. -- Isaiah 7:9.**

Isaiah's faith was in God. Armstrong–Yoshitake's faith is in God and its core values. Those core values are fairness, honesty, and loyalty. Larry Daugherty, Tom Grubka, Cam Spence and I were there when we signed the contract with Warren Wilson. Larry has conveyed these core values to the newly hired Armstrong–Yoshitake employees like Tom Hyatt, Tim Jones, Chad Baker and Rex Scare. They live these core values when dealing with Warren Wilson.

29.

R.H.I.P

You have stumbled upon a tragic story which involves yours truly. Armstrong International had just introduced Armstrong Steam University on its web page. The purpose of Armstrong Steam University is to impart knowledge on steam, condensate, and air through a series of courses. If you feel brave, you can attempt to pass a series of tests. If you pass all 6 tests with 100% you are rewarded with an Armstrong University T-shirt. On the T-shirt is our famous character and web page course guide, Armey Steamstrong, who looks a little bit like Albert Einstein. These T-shirts are in high demand. Everybody wants one!

One day I found myself at the doorstep of our Web Master, Pam Blasius. "Hi Pam. Could I have one of the Armstrong Steam University T-shirts?"

"Uh, sure David. You know you are supposed to take the tests before I give you a shirt."

"Yeah, I know. I'm going to take the tests when I get home. I just thought I would get the shirt now."

"Uh, OK. What size do you need?"

"Why don't you give me a large?"

One week later I received a letter in the mail from David Collins, an Armstrong Representative. The letter read: 'The grapevine has it that the Chief Operating Officer has received an Armstrong Steam University T-shirt without passing the test. While I was in the Army we had a saying; R.H.I.P.- - *Rank Has Its Privileges*. David Armstrong is known for storytelling throughout the halls of Armstrong, does he also want to be known for R.H.I.P?'

> *Power does not kill; it permits suicide.*
> *Earl Shorris, writer*

THE MORAL OF THE STORY

1. **"Lead us not into temptation"**.
Remember this story I wrote in my first book, <u>Managing By Storying Around</u>? The morals to that story warned people not to be tempted to do things they knew were wrong. I took advantage of my authority and forced Pam to give me a T-shirt. That was wrong. Bravo David Collins for having the courage to set my moral compass back on target. I went astray. We as leaders are not perfect; we need brave souls to keep us from being corrupted by the power we possess.

2. **I knew better.**
I apologized to Pam Blasius and to all the other people who have taken the tests and passed them. This story has been written to apologize to all who were cheated by my actions, and to give Pam Blasius the authority to refuse to give an Armstrong Steam University T-shirt to anyone who has <u>not</u> taken and passed all the tests with a 100% score.

3. **The end.**
Wait a minute. The ending to this story has not been told. Yes, I returned the Armstrong Steam University T-shirt to Pam Blasius.

30.
LET'S PRAY

This story begins on the Internet. I had just downloaded my e-mail and was scanning through a list of letters when I found a letter from David Dykstra, the Financial Officer for Armstrong Machine Works.

It was the end of month and I wanted to see financials for that division so I clicked on his letter. I was surprised when I read the subject line in the email. It read "Armstrong Prayer Hot Line." The letter was announcing the next monthly meeting for the Armstrong Prayer Hot Line. It just so happened that Tom Morris, General Counsel for Armstrong International, and I were in Michigan that week, so we decided to attend.

Tom and I were pleased to see the number of Armstrong employees waiting for David to lead them in prayer. David begins:

> "Let's pray." David bows his head, as did we all.

> "Our Father who art in heaven, we pray to you today to give you all glory for you are the Creator and the Father. We **praise** you and worship you, and only you. We also pray to you to give **thanks** for the grace you have given us. And finally, we pray to **ask** for your help. We have many loved ones who are sick, who are in the hospital, who need your help. The families of these people also need your strength and guidance."

David then begins to list over 20 names of people who needed a prayer due to sickness or deaths in their family. A few others in the group also gave a prayer of thanks and asked for help for their loved ones. When the last employee had said their prayer, David said Amen.

Why pray if God knows all things?

THE MORAL OF THE STORY

1. **Prayer is designed for our benefit, not God's:**
Prayer is not designed for furnishing God with the knowledge of what we need, but it is designed as a confession to Him of our utter dependence upon Him.

2. **Prayer always works because it strengthens us and our relationship with God.**
Prayer is one way in which we commune with our Heavenly Father. The more we communicate with Him, the better we know Him.

3. **How do you pray to God?**
First, you give **praise**, glory, worship, and adore Him. Second, you give **thanks** for what He has given you -- no matter how terrible things are. Third, you **ask** for things you need. He may not always give you what you ask, but he always hears you.

31.

DEAR FRIEND

As the time approaches 12 noon, we walk to the parking lot to drive to lunch. When we reach our guest's car he finds a piece of paper under the wipers on the windshield. It reads:

> *Dear Friend:*
> *"I couldn't help but notice the SUV you are driving is equipped with a brand of tires that have been recalled by the manufacturer based on safety concerns. I recognize this vehicle as being a rental car. The rental car industry has had a difficult time in replacing these tires because the vehicles are being used too often. You can help by pointing this out to the rental car company when you return your vehicle. Until then, be careful and drive safely."*
> *James D. Beach, Manager, Safety & Environmental Health, Armstrong Service.*

A danger foreseen is half avoided.
--1000 proverbs

THE MORAL OF THE STORY

1. **Better face a danger than always be in fear.—1000 Proverbs.**
This rental car company lives in fear every day that an accident may happen due to these tires. Are they putting profit ahead of safety. Do you think James Beach, the Safety Manager for Armstrong Service, would allow profits to come ahead of safety? No Way! The proof — he lives safety everyday even in parking lots at Armstrong Service.

2. **Dear friend.**
Our guest that day was a <u>competitor</u> of Armstrong. James left a very favorable memory with our competitor about Armstrong. This guest folded up this message (story) and put it in his shirt pocket. Now let's suppose our guest had been a potential customer. Do you think James' safety message would have helped Armstrong Service get the job? <u>Only if safety is a concern</u>!

32.

GUARDIAN ANGEL

In December of 1998, on a cold, wet and windy morning, while working for a former employee I was forced by circumstance and against my better judgment into dragging decking material on the roof of the new department store addition at North-Park Mall in Dallas.

Most of the employees assumed we would be rained-out once again and decided not to waste their time in coming to work. The crane operator was one of those who decided to stay home that day. No operator meant no crane. Without a crane you cannot hang iron. Not hanging iron meant that my partner and I, the connectors, either went home along with the rest of the erection crew, or we stayed behind and worked for Junior (who happened to be the owner's son) to whom the job of foreman had been handed on a silver platter. Based on this, we knew in advance that we would be given whatever crappy job was left over.

It was two weeks before Christmas. I was raising four children by myself at the time. We had been rained out from work three days last week and four days the week before. In fact, because of adverse weather, it had been a full month since we last worked a complete 40 hours in any week. Money was tight. I'd already used my meager savings trying to keep the electricity turned on and paying rent. I was determined to give my children the best Christmas I could, no matter what the cost!

The boss's kid could care less if we stayed; in fact he would prefer it if we all went home. He was on salary and would get his money regardless! Since a handful of us were willing to work, mostly members of the erection crew like myself (the majority of the people who worked for "Junior" hated him and were more than happy to go home with their two hours of show-up pay), Junior was forced to stay on the job with us.

"If you boys want to stay and work today then you're going to drag deck," he informed us, thinking this would make us give up and go back home. Each sheet of decking weighed 310 pounds.

In the best of conditions, dragging deck is the single most dangerous job an ironworker performs. The metal sheets that comprise the deck are moved into position, the edges lapped over the previous sheet and then "spot-welded" into place, a temporary method of holding it down and preventing it from flying off until all the deck has been placed into position, at which time it can be properly welded. As new sheets are moved over the top of these spot-welded sheets, the edge of the sheet being carried can accidentally catch on the sheet below it. If enough force is present, the sheet that was spot-welded into place rips loose and the ironworker who is unfortunate enough to be standing on top of it at that moment falls to the nearest completed level below him. Oftentimes one of the sheets falls after him. If the fall doesn't kill him, the 60, 80, or in this case 300-pound razor blade that falls behind him will, unless he is lucky.

High winds also play a factor in the danger of performing this task. The 4 feet wide by 30 feet long sheeting acts like a sail and catches the wind. Many times an ironworker has been literally blown off the roof of a building by the wind while attempting to move sheeting.

Because of the inherent danger of this kind of work, efforts are <u>usually</u> made to place the stacks of deck sheeting as close as possible to where they belong, thus minimizing the dangers associated with their movement.

As the connectors on this job, my partner and I had been the ones who helped to place these bundles of decking up on the roof earlier last week. We both observed the length of the sheets in this bundle and realized that the only place these could possibly go were over the center atrium, almost a football fields' length away from where they flew them up to. My partner, who had the radio, called the Superintendent and asked him to "fly the hook back up here, this bundle of decking needed to be landed way over there, not here". The Superintendent replied to my partner that if he wanted his opinion he'd have asked him for it, and if he wanted to keep his job he'd better keep his mouth shut and mind his own business! That's the spot "Junior" wanted it set! If that's what "Junior" wanted, that's what "Junior" would get!

My partner and I grinned at each other; we had figured out what was going on. The Superintendent resented the fact that the boss's kid had been dumped off on him at this job. He was playing a game called "Give him enough rope to hang himself", and when the time came to give answer to why all the work was so far behind schedule, the Superintendent was going to make it known that it was because of decisions made by the boss's kid.

Now here we were, my partner and I, having to drag this deck that we knew shouldn't have been placed there in the first place! Needless to say, we were both a little ticked off about it! We each grabbed the end of a sheet and turned it up on edge to slide it over the decking at a 45 degree angle to reduce the chances of it getting caught or snared on the edge of the decking that had been "temporaried" into place.

Junior saw us moving the first sheet and started yelling at us. "You two are wasting mine and the company's time! If the both of you can't **each** drag two sheets at a time **by yourselves**, then we don't need you and I'll send you your check in the mail!"

With the wind blowing such as it was and the deck slippery from rain, I knew better! My partner knew better as well. Both of us should have walked off the job that morning and never looked back. Unfortunately, the pressures of the holiday's were upon us and we were both determined to make a full day's pay, come hell or high-water!

We attached a set of Vice-Grip C-clamps onto one corner of two sheets corrugated together and tied a rope around it. This was dangerous and both of us knew it. Special clamps known as "dogs" are made for this purpose, and unless the metal rips out, the dog will not come loose! Unfortunately, the contractor was too cheap to buy them.

Can you imagine dragging 600 pounds behind you by rope? Obviously, you cannot perform this type of maneuver while standing erect. You must lean forward considerably and use the weight of the object attached by rope as a counter balance against falling. To compound this problem, the decking on which we walked was enamel coated, smooth, and wet. In order to get this much weight moving you had to lean hard and pull. Once the sheeting you were tugging on broke free, you had to continually increase your speed to keep it moving without dropping the front edge, which would in turn cause it to catch and rip loose the sheeting you were standing on.

It was a dangerous thing that we were doing! We knew this, but we felt that our experience in this type of work would prevent us from being injured. By the time we reached the end of the decked surface to the opening where the sheets we were towing would cover, we were almost at **a full run**! When we were within a foot or so from the open edge we would jump to the side so as not to get hit by the sheets we had in tow, which could knock our footing out from beneath us. The decking would slide a few inches out past the edge under its own inertia, at which time we would jerk backward on the rope, which dislodged the clamp from the sheets and stopped their forward travel.

As for the perimeter safety cables tensioned along the edge of the opening being an obstacle for us, we needn't worry. This contractor for which we worked did not want to waste the time or money in erecting any kind of safety cables. Fall protection? Safety harnesses? The mention of any such thing brought humiliation and scorn to anyone who suggested any such thing! The attitude was, and still is even today, that "if you are afraid of heights and think that you need to wear some kind of fall protection equipment then you must not be much of an ironworker!" The mere suggestion of any such device was enough to get you sent home with a pink slip in your hand!

We had carefully orchestrated these maneuvers around ten times each. We had our rhythm down pact. On my 11th approach as I came within a foot or so from the edge of the roof opening at full speed with 600 pounds in tow behind me and was about to jump over to the side and allow the sheets to go past me, the clamp came loose! My forward momentum and the force that I exerted **should**

have hurled my body forward over the unprotected edge. There was no time for me to react, and I cannot take credit for what happened! My reflexes, your reflexes, or anyone's reflexes, for that matter; are not fast enough to allow recovery in the way that I did on that day.

My body went suddenly erect as if an invisible hand had reached out and grabbed me by the collar of my shirt and pulled me upright. My feet became firmly anchored and **set** on the slippery surface on which I was standing to such an extent that even the 600 pounds of steel sliding into the back of my heels could not dislodge my feet from where they were planted. I stood there, looking down at the concrete 60 feet below me, rigid, steady and sure!

I was alive! Adrenaline was pumping through my body as a cold chill swept across my back and shoulders, but just as suddenly as the clamp had come loose from the decking, my heart began to beat out a slow and relaxed cadence. A smile found its way onto my face. I recognized the voice inside my ear whispering to me, "Be still, and do not fear!" Over the sound of this whisper I became aware of my partner screaming out my name and exclaiming out loud, "JAMES!...Oh my God"!

My partner, also named James (we were known as the James Gang) who I will hereafter refer to as Jim, described for anyone who would listen to him the events he saw and the order in which they happened. He saw the clamp pop loose and go flying ahead of me as the elasticity of the rope gave way to the laws of physics, propelling the clamp as if fired from a slingshot. He saw me pitch forward as if I were about to dive head first into the concrete 60 feet below me. He saw my body, suddenly made erect, and stop as if I had come into contact with a brick wall! He examined the marks left in the heels of my boots where the edge of the metal sheeting sliced into the hard rubber of the soles but did not push me at all. He saw the smile on my face as I turned to look at him and he knew, as did I, this was the product of divine intervention.

Jim was not a Christian. I had only recently started going to church again after more than 20 years of avoiding it. My children had expressed interest in the idea of going to church and I felt that it was the right thing to do.

Jim broke into a chorus of a song that I remembered from my childhood and I joined him. Together we sang these words. "All night, All day, Angels watching over me my Lord...."

We worked the remainder of that day completely unperturbed by "Junior" and his nasty comments. If he wanted to fire us, so be it! Nothing could replace the awe and wonder that was contained within us. We'd both witnessed and been party to something on that day that could only be described as miraculous!

> *If anything can go wrong, it will.*
> *--Murphy's Law*

The Moral Of The Story

1. **Do what I say, not what I do.**
   "As your Safety Director, it would be hypocritical for me to tell you that I have never violated any safety rules because I was in a hurry, or because I felt pressured by a supervisor to do so." I am sure you picked up on several things, which you recognize as being unsafe. I knew better and so do you. Self-manage your safety and stay alive.

2. **One million man-hours with no lost-time injures, and only <u>ONE</u> recordable injury in four years!**
   You and now I are fortunate to work for a company that cares about you as a person. Armstrong Service, Inc's (ASI) commitment to you and the well being of your family is a matter of public record. Armstrong is proud of you, their valued employee. ASI will not put your life on the line for the sake of greater productivity. This was not the case with my previous employer. ASI will always provide the tools and materials you need to do your job safely and the resources to learn the best method of doing it.

3. **If ASI, or an ASI supervisor ever fails to provide you with the proper equipment, or training, or asks you to do something that is unsafe; you must call me!**
   I am grateful for the position I have here with Armstrong Service where I have the opportunity to make a difference.

James D. Beach
Manager Safety & Environmental Health
David M. Armstrong

STORIES
TO BOOST
CREATIVITY

CHAPTER 7

33.
GRANDPA'S GIFT

Grandpa quietly sat in his chair as he listened to the instructor talk about steam. For the last two days Armstrong University professors had shared knowledge on steam. Throughout the two days many gifts had been given to the students. The final gift was in a little yellow box full of crayons. Grandpa looked at the box and didn't understand why he would be getting this gift. Wasn't he too old to be playing with crayons?

The President of Armstrong Steam University spoke. "You probably wonder why we gave you a box of crayons. We think you should take them back to your company or department and let your guests sign in with them."

Grandpa remembered seeing the crayons in Armstrong's lobby, affectionately called 'Home Sweet Home'. A professor broke grandpa's thoughts.

"Our Chief Operating Officer thinks you may also need a gift for your son, daughter, or grandchild."

When grandpa heard this, a smile appeared. He thought, "They really have thought of everything."

After class Grandpa approached the professor. "I have a problem. I have two grandchildren and I can't take one box of crayons home."

"Here," said the professor, "take this second box of crayons."

Grandpa smiled again and shook his head in disbelief. "Your (CSO) Chief Storytelling Officer really

STORIES TO BOOST CREATIVITY   111

understands what it's like to be away from your family. Every time I come home, my grandchildren ask me what I brought them. Sometimes I don't have time to buy them a gift. This time Armstrong did my shopping for me."

> *Do not do what is already done.*
> *—Terrance 190-159 B.C.*

THE MORAL OF THE STORY

1. **A gift cannot be valued if it is not understood.**
If we had given the crayons and not told our students how to use them, they would have found the nearest wastebasket. Don't assume your creative ideas will be understood. Help explain them so they succeed and get used.

2. **Before a brilliant person looks great...**they must look foolish to the crowd.
I'm sure the Armstrong Steam University students thought I was crazy giving them crayons, that is, until they were told how to use the crayons. I'm sure many Armstrongers thought I was foolish giving crayons to customers. One of the best ways to get a new customer or keep a customer happy is through their family. Thus, we give the gift of crayons.

3. **Is this a bribe?**
Read my story "Bribes" in How To Turn Your Company's Parables Into Profit. Armstrong received no orders or favors for the crayons and other gifts. If I were a student, I would not be afraid to tell everyone how I got the free crayons. Would you? Crayons have little monetary value—$1.98.

The student's company could benefit from the crayons if used in their lobby. The other gifts were a hat, duffle bag, Cross pen, book of Armstrong stories, audio CD of Armstrong stories and a denim shirt.

34.

A HORSE THIEF

It may be hard to believe, but there really is a horse thief in this twentieth century. It all began in a little sleepy village called Armstrong. Pat Gillem owned a horse named Flint. Flint was a spirited horse, and could often be seen rearing back on his hind legs. Pat is a horse trainer, but also has another job working as a welder at Armstrong International. One day while walking through his department, Pat noticed a pile of scrap. The scrap had taken the shape of a man. Pat asked himself, "Wouldn't it be fun to take scrap parts and weld them together to make animals and people?" That day at break he picked up some scrap pieces and began his welding. Before long, Pat's artwork could be found throughout the village for others to enjoy.

One day, while touring the factory, I noticed one of Pat's creations on the floor. It was a horse rearing back on its hind legs with a man riding it. The man had one of his hands in the air like you would see at a rodeo. Pat had even taken some frayed rope and used it for the horse's tail and mane. The ears were pointed straight up, and it looked like a spirited horse as it tried to throw its rider. I quickly bent over and picked it up. I began walking to my office.

Some eighty steps later I heard someone shout, "HORSE THIEF!! What are you doing with that horse?"

I stopped dead in my tracks and turned around. There was Pat with a smile on his face. "I created that after my horse, Flint."

"It's beautiful", I replied. "I really like the way you used Armstrong products and parts. My wife likes to ride horses, and I thought it would look good with the rest of our art. I didn't think you would mind if I took it since it was made out of scrap."

"I would be honored if you would take it home. I am just having some fun with you, David. It's not everyday you find a horse thief in the twentieth century."

> Creative minds develop exciting products.

THE MORAL OF THE STORY

1. **Go instead where there is no path and blaze a trail.**
I've instructed Pat and his foreman, Tom Miller, to create five more people out of scrap. I want to present these as awards to the top salespeople. It beats giving a plaque—that's boring. After all, the award is made out of the very product the salespeople are selling. It's much more meaningful. We could even use Pat's art as prized awards for companies and employees with 10, 15, or 20 years of service.

2. **If passion drives, let reason hold the reins. — Benjamin Franklin.**
Pat needs a lot of passion to create art with his hands, but he has enough reason to practice his hobby on his own time and with unusable company scrap.

3. **Passion demands Passion.—Tom Peters.**
We, as leaders, need to show passion when employees show passion. It's supporting. I always enjoy finding people who are creative and passionate. Pat could be good at designing new products. Hire artists who are creative to think of new products.

35.
R.I.P.

The tombstone read "Born 1959 - Died 1999". The Armstrong family could not believe it had been 40 years. Tom Quake and Tom Rockwell were good friends of the deceased and were standing by as the pallbearers. Forty years may not seem like a long time. It's much too early for a person to die, but this piece of literature, the purger catalog died of old age.

    Tom Rockwell and Tom Quake were trying to breathe life back into the Armstrong Refrigeration Purger. Besides designing new products and finding new distribution outlets, they knew they needed to develop new literature. They decided to get creative in the way they would introduce the literature. They put an announcement out which was a picture of a tombstone with bold letters **R.I.P.** On the tombstone was the quote "May the dead guys rest in peace." This quote had become well-known within Armstrong and its sales force because the men on the cover page of the purger catalog were from the 1940's. The men looked to be well in their 40's or 50's at that time, so they would be well over 100 today. **R.I.P.**

> *Better late than never.*
>   *--Latin Proverb*

THE MORAL OF THE STORY

1. **Better late than never.**
Not always true. At one time Armstrong was the leader in refrigeration with purgers. Just recently, one of our main competitors sold its business for 29 million dollars. We lost this market by not staying focused on it.

2. **"Our Toilet-paper Secret".**
Remember this story in my book <u>Managing By Storying Around?</u> I talked about Rich Hitz having a great idea so he wrote it on a roll of toilet-paper to get the President's attention. This story sounds familiar. Tom Rockwell and Tom Quake had a new piece of literature for the purger and wanted people to read it. It was not the most popular product at Armstrong, and so both Tom's decided to get creative and send a fax out with a picture of a tombstone which had in bold letters **R.I.P.** At the bottom, details were given about the deceased, the services, the pallbearers and the memorials. All this information led the reader back to the Armstrong International Refrigeration group, to our web site, to product champions (pallbearers), and, of course, to the new piece of literature.

3. **And that's the rest of the story.**
Yes, my stories do sound familiar. Many of them have a surprise ending. I do that to keep your attention. Maybe you recall my stories, "A Piece of Fun" and "The Blimp"? Stories with a surprise ending are fun to read. Literature with a creative introduction gets read.

R.I.P

May the Dead Guys Rest in Peace

In Memory of

The Purger Bulletin No. 702-C

Born - Bulletin 700, August 1959
Died - Bulletin 702-C, September 1999
Three Rivers, MI

Services
Private services held by the
Armstrong Refrigeration Group
September, 1999

Bearers
Tom Rockwell
Tom Quake

Internment
Into the archives of Armstrong International, Inc.

Memorials
May be found on the Armstrong Web Site
www.armstrong-intl.com

36.

COLOR INSIDE THE LINES

The crayon fit tightly between the student's fingers as she began to press firmly on the paper. Carefully she printed each letter of her name between the lines. When she finished, she checked the spelling of her name. Yep, S-Y-L-V-I-A in bright orange was correct. She handed the sheet of paper and box of crayons to the next student.

Duane carefully chose purple as his favorite color and began to print his name. Duane had trouble staying within the lines. He would obviously have to practice more. He then handed it to the next student.

"Here Dave, sign your name."

"Dave also grabbed a purple crayon and printed his first letter—D, then he grabbed a green crayon and printed A, followed by an orange V, and another dark green E. He then chose purple for S, green for H, and when he was all done he had a rainbow of colors spelling Dave Shutler. Several more students signed before the last student took the sheet of names back to the Armstrong University professor.

"Here is the list of names interested in dinner tonight."

"Thank you."

> *Smiling and laughing are free, easy to learn, no experience required.*

THE MORAL OF THE STORY

1. **I have it on good authority that each of you were a seven-year old at one time.**
Let that child come out. Dave Shutler, who used all the crayons in this story, did just that. And get this......Dave Shutler was a Colonel in the United States Air Force. If that isn't shocking enough, he is also a lawyer! He served as a Member for the Air Force of the Judge Advocate General Corps for over 20 years. He is now the Director of Government Business for Armstrong Service government procurement. Dave didn't just use one crayon, he used many different crayons. A real sign of a playful spirit and creative soul. I'll bet Armstrong lawyers are more creative than your marketing people. Any bets?

2. **"Children enter school as question marks, and leave as periods."— Neil Postman is right.**
When we all go to school, our creativity is high, we are full of ideas, nothing is impossible. By the time we graduate, I daresay from grade school, most of our creativity is gone. We have been taught by those non-creative people, that's right, **adults**, that you just don't behave that way. Here's to bringing back the Tooth Fairy, leprechauns, Santa Claus, stitch fairies, the Easter Bunny, and yes, even crayons. Can you remember the creativity you had when you first started working? Get it back and practice it every day, and if crayons help you do that, use them!

Armstrong

Important

**ARMSTRONG STEAM UNIVERSITY
LOG SHEET
TUESDAY DINNER ATTENDANCE**

Please, print your name and company as you would like it to appear on your certificate. **Check** the appropriate **box** below for **dinner attendance** and **circle shirt size.** Thank you.

Print Your Name and Company	Dinner Will be Attending	Dinner Will **not** be attending
Name: Steve Raby Company: Wallace Thermo Shirt Size: S M L (XL)	Yes	
Name: DAVE SHUTLER Company: AST Shirt Size: S M L (XL)	Yes	
Name: DUANE SNYDER Company: Shirt Size: S M L (XL)	Yes	
Name: Mark Peterson Company: ConServ Inc. Shirt Size: S M (L) XL	Yes.	

seminar log
08/23/99

STORIES
TO HONOR
PARTNERSHIPS

CHAPTER 8

37.

CLANKETY CLANK! CLANKETY CLANK!

It was hot and muggy that night. Windows were open for any cool breeze, as people lay in their beds fast asleep. When the cool breeze came from the north, the hot night began to cool down, making it easier to sleep. The curtains flapped as the wind blew through the window, and a noise in the near distance could be heard -- *Clankety Clank, Clankety Clank.* When the window curtains stopped flapping, the noise went away. Soon a cool breeze blew through the window again, disturbing the curtains -- *Clankety Clank, Clankety Clank.* People began to wake up.

"What is that noise?"

Clankety Clank, Clankey Clank.

"There it is again! "Where's that coming from?"

The awakened people looked out their windows and there across the street they found the cause of the noise. Armstrong International had just installed seven flag poles and as the wind blew the flags the metal fasteners would bang against the flag poles.

That next morning Bill Hartman, foreman for the punch press department, began to receive phone calls from his neighbors.

"Bill, did you hear that noise last night? It woke me up! Somebody needs to change the fasteners on the flags poles at Armstrong International. Your company is keeping everybody up."

Bill quickly notified management. That same day metal fasteners were replaced with plastic, which did not make that terrible noise, *Clankety Clank, Clankety Clank.*

A good neighbor is a company's best friend.

THE MORAL OF THE STORY

1. **Don't look for the bad; look for the good in your neighbors.**
Our neighbors never complain about the traffic our company creates. Our neighbors never complain about Armstrong International's Christmas celebrations, which include some 7,000 people near their homes. Our neighbors never complain about the loud speaker going off late in the evening during the second shift. Our neighbors never complain about the noise the factory makes. So, when Armstrong neighbors complain about the noise our flagpoles make, we are happy to fix the problem.

2. **"The price of greatness is responsibility"** — **Winston Churchill.**
In 1996, the Better Business Bureau of Western Michigan honored Armstrong International with the award, "1996 Best in Community Service." How can we not be responsible to our fellow neighbors after receiving this award? This is who we are; this is why we won the award!!

3. **Bill Hartman is an Armstrong ambassador for community service . . .**
Are you?

38.

LAUREN'S FIRST VISIT WITH SANTA

For several weeks, Lauren has shyly admitted that she knew what she wanted to ask Santa for Christmas. I've asked her what she wants, but she has refused to tell me. (Later, I found out that she told her older sister, Brittany, but made her "pinky swear" not to ask Santa for the same thing or to tell anyone.) Anyway, I had forgotten these earlier conversations, and watched as Lauren somewhat hesitantly approached Santa. With her head slightly bowed and a hand to her face because she is shy with strangers, I could tell she was struggling to approach and talk to Santa. She did sit on his lap but I couldn't hear a word that was said between them. Soon Santa was nodding and Lauren stood up beside him as he reached for his belt. Tucked into his belt was a gold bell tied on to a cord of red and gold. He reached out and hung the bell around her neck and Lauren smiled one of her biggest most precious smiles. Tears came to my eyes as I watched her walk off the stage. I asked her what she had asked Santa for. She proudly displayed her treasure and told me, "I asked for a bell from his sleigh". "That's what you wanted from Santa for Christmas?" She turned her beaming smile back on, bent her head down in that cute shy way and nodded. Is there anything more wonderful in the world than the feeling you get when a child is truly happy? Thank you Armstag for all your hard work. I appreciate all you have given with your time and talents to make this a very Merry Christmas for the Cummings family.

Partnerships among employees.

THE MORAL OF THE STORY

1. **"I wanted to tell you my heartwarming story about my daughter Lauren (8) and her visit with Santa".**
Last weekend was the annual **Armstag** Children's Christmas party. For those who don't know what **Armstag** is, I will tell you. It is a club for the employees of Armstrong Divisions in Three Rivers, Michigan. It is run by elected employees who volunteer their time for special company events. Its purpose is to raise money and support <u>employee </u>gatherings. "I appreciate all you have given with your time and talents to make this a very Merry Christmas for the Cummings family."

2. **Armstag is a partnership between each Armstrong employee in Three Rivers.**
Sometimes it even involves an employee's child. Rex Cummings' daughter, Lauren, will remember this day for a long time. Rex may remember Lauren's *beaming* smile even longer. Partnerships need success stories such as this one if they wish to survive.

3. **The apple doesn't fall far from the tree.**
Rex Cummings' father, Carl, retired from Armstrong International. Another partnership between the Armstrong family and the Cummings family—a partnership two generations strong.

>Authors: Rex Cummings
>And
>David M. Armstrong

39.
TWINS

"I hear two heartbeats!" said the Doctor.

"TWO!!" repeated Michelle.

"Yes, two heartbeats. Congratulations! You're going to have twins for the second time."

"Will I have the same problem I had with my first set of twins?"

"Do you mean giving birth prematurely?"

"Yes."

"I think there is a good possibility, so I want you to take it easy at work and at home."

The summer came and passed. Four months before Michelle was due, the doctors informed her that she would have to remain in bed to prevent a premature birth. Pat Reed and Deb Schull went into action.

"We need to find a way to feed Michelle's family. Let's make up a calendar several months in advance and each of the Armstrongers can take a day when they will cook a meal," offered Pat.

"That's a great idea! We also need to have food runners. Let's pick four Armstrongers who will deliver the food so Michelle doesn't have someone different coming to her house each day," added Deb.

"Who's going to clean the house and keep up with the laundry?" asked another.

Before long, Michelle's family was receiving home-cooked meals and on weekends co-workers were doing her household chores.

True Armstrong!

THE MORAL OF THE STORY

1. **A good partnership is not built in a day.**
Pat, Deb, and Michelle have worked at Armstrong for 20 years. Through the years their friendship has grown strong.

2. **Partnerships are not just for suppliers.**
You have partnerships within your company, which can be seen among your employees. Pat, Deb, and all the other Armstrongers have a strong partnership with Michelle—some call it *family*.

3. **True friends remain loyal in times of need.**
Don't you wish you worked with people like Deb and Pat? True Armstrong! Our employees never cease to amaze me. Helping a fellow Armstronger in time of need reveals the friendship that exists at Armstrong International. Can you say the same about your company?

40.

BOWLING IN ENGLAND

Dedicated to: Joe Meany, Kim Stuart, Roger Hathaway, Roy Minett, Roy North, David Webb, Mark Pickering, Russell Thorndale, and Hadyn Cooling

---

This story has a happy ending. It began with a visit to England. Paul Knight and Tom Rockwell from Armstrong-Lynnwood, and Paul Holliday and myself from Armstrong International, were visiting Caradon Mira, Ltd. We had been meeting all day, and with the five-hour time change, we were becoming tired by the end of the day. Mark Pickering, Manager and Director, then said that we would go to the local bowling alley at 7:00 p.m. We would bowl for an hour, and then go out for a light dinner. We were all given a chance to return to the hotel and change from our suits and ties into casual attire. Once we arrived at the bowling alley, teams were drawn up, and the bowling began. Much to my surprise, Tom Rockwell couldn't help himself and had to make another stupid bet. You remember Tom's story titled, "It Never Rains on the Golf Course," in my latest book, <u>Once Told, They're Gold.</u> This bowling bet was for one dozen golf balls. We had a lot of fun that night and made several new friends as we bowled. Here was proof that people who play together, work well together. Afterwards at dinner, a lot of heckling, laughing, and abuse followed about how well each of us played. Oh, I forgot to mention the best part of the story. Tom Rockwell **lost** and owes me a dozen HP2 Titleist® golf balls. I told you the story had a happy ending.

Pursue leaders who make partnerships fun.

THE MORAL OF THE STORY

1. **If you want a strong partnership, try becoming business friends first.**
Mark Pickering understands this. I can't think of a better way to break the ice between strangers than to go bowling. Very quickly, we all realized just how competitive we were, and how much fun we have picking on one another. I felt much closer to each of the Caradon people after that night of bowling. I'm sure I'm not alone. A great way to start a partnership.

2. **I'm not afraid to say it . . .**
I will probably remember the night I bowled with all my friends at Caradon, more than the products we discussed. Yes, I know, the products are why we went to Caradon in hopes of creating more business for Armstrong and Caradon. I also know the same secret that Mark knows. Business is done between friends. In one hour of bowling, Mark made it possible for the people at Caradon and Armstrong to become closer friends. Now, that's what I call partnership--I mean PARTNERSHIP!

® Registered by Accushment

41.
A PENNY

We had recently entered into an agreement with Ferguson Enterprises, Inc. to distribute Armstrong products. Tom Grubka, the General Manager at Armstrong in Three Rivers, was anxious to show good faith and to reciprocate by buying tooling from them. Ferguson had purchased South Bend Supply which years ago had been a major supplier to Armstrong Machine Works. Tom called Joyce Clay, the Manufacture Resource Officer.

"Joyce, I'd like to start using Ferguson as a supplier for tooling again."

"OK," Joyce responded, "but every time I've had them quote on items, they've always been one of the higher quotes."

"Well, work with them. See what you can do about it."

Joyce met with Stan Bennett, the outside sales Rep from Ferguson. "Stan, Armstrong wants to be a true partner, but at the same time I'm charged to keep our disposable tooling cost within budget. When I put out quotes in the past, Ferguson has always been the high bidder. Here are some examples. What can we do about this?"

Stan went back and talked to his boss, Tom Noble. Together they agreed to increase the discount on tooling to Armstrong. Joyce began purchasing more items from

Ferguson. One day she received a fax acknowledging an order for three different types of inserts. The price had been corrected on the first two items ordered. Delivery date had been noted. The third and last item showed a price of 1¢. Often Joyce will put 1¢ on an item if she doesn't have correct pricing in her computer. The acknowledgment was signed by Reid Kipp, the inside sales person, and constituted a contract. When Joyce received the fax she looked at the 1¢ price— not corrected, she picked up the phone and dialed Reid.

"Hi Reid. Thanks for acknowledging my purchase order number 301204, but do you really want to sell me the VNMG Insert for a penny a piece? I know I told you Ferguson had to be competitive, but 1¢?"

"What?!" Reid said, "Thanks for calling. Let me get you the right price. I'm glad you caught my mistake and won't hold me to it."

It's never a good deal when only one party thinks it is.

THE MORAL OF THE STORY

1. **True partners look out for each other.**
Joyce didn't want to take advantage of her vendor. She knows it has to be a win-win situation. She needs Ferguson to stay in business to supply our tooling.

2. **Point out mistakes in a friendly way.**
Don't embarrass your partner. We all make mistakes. Joyce made a friend that day. In the future, Reid would set

other customers aside to find and deliver a tool Joyce needed on the very next day.

3. **Friends make great partners.**
If Joyce gives Reid an Armstrong purchase order and Reid can give her a lower price, he will. Why? Respect and friendship.

# STORIES
TO HONOR
QUALITY AND SERVICE

CHAPTER 9

42.
IF YOU BUILD IT, YOU WILL BUY IT!

Has your Company committed the unforgivable sin? What will your answer be when this story is over? This is my story about promoting Armstrong steam trap *surveys* as a way to improve our customer's energy efficiency. We did this same *survey* on our own steam trap population.

Today, if you walk through Armstrong's factories, you will notice that each installed steam trap has been tagged and identified as working or failed. The failed steam traps are replaced with new Armstrong Inverted Bucket Steam Traps. They are checked to insure that we have no steam leaks. If we believe the message we give our customers (Inverted Bucket Steam Traps can be a large energy saver), then we should practice what we preach and save energy in our own factories. Each time we buy a new company, we should make sure to install Armstrong products in that company. We must also use the newly acquired company's products in Armstrong divisions.

> Customers are reassured when they see you using your own products.

THE MORAL OF THE STORY

1. **If you were an Armstrong customer what would you think if you saw Armstrong's factories using a competitor's products?**
You would think the quality of these competitive brands is better than Armstrong. We have many customers who walk through our factories on tours. Let's make sure we give them the right message by allowing them, no, pointing out to them, that we use our own products. This may seem like a little thing, but it will reassure the customer that they made the right choice buying Armstrong.

2. **You want to speed up the testing of Armstrong's new products.**
Why not test them in Armstrong's factories? It's quicker because there is no delay waiting for customer approval. You can also see the products <u>every</u> day. You can experience the problems with installation — first hand. You can make modifications, quickly and inexpensively. Testing new products can be simpler and quicker if you test them in your own company.

3. **You want to know if Armstrong products are easy to install or repair?**
Listen to *your* maintenance department as they install or repair *your* products. Do you have the guts to try this? Be prepared for an ear full!!

4. **You want to know if Armstrong products are too expensive?**

If you hear your *own* management complain about the high price as they replace less costly competitive brands, your price is too high. Enough said!

43.

VENT WIRE

𝒯his story begins when Mike Osterloh, Construction Services Manager for Armstrong Service, Inc. is at a customer's plant. Armstrong Service, Inc. had just been awarded the contract to replace the customer's steam traps and all the piping around them. After installing the first 200 Armstrong Steam Traps, Mike noticed that most of the traps were not working. This couldn't be! These were Armstrong's <u>Inverted Bucket</u> Steam Traps, famous for their quality and long life. He decided to approach the Project Manager.

"I think we have a problem with the Armstrong Steam Traps. We have installed two hundred traps but some don't seem to be working? I'm going to call the factory and tell them that we have to take them back."

"This is not a good way to start a new project," answered the Project Manager. "I appreciate your honesty."

"We intend to do this project right, that's what you're paying us for."

"It would have been easy for Armstrong to not tell us about the bad traps and try to hide the problem." Replied the customer. A smile comes to his face.

Shortly thereafter, Mike called the factory informing us of the problems with the Inverted Bucket Steam Traps. He took one of the Steam Traps out of installation and returned it to the factory where it was cut open. What we found was the vent wire which was positioned through the orifice hole of the bucket had been installed improperly. The vent wire was binding on the bucket and would not allow the bucket to go up and down, which was its normal mode of operation. Additional training on proper installation of the vent wire was given so this would not happen again.

> Bad news early, is better than bad news late.

THE MORAL OF THE STORY

1. **Don't kill the messenger bearing bad news.**
Most of us have said this once in our life, but how many of you practice it? Instead of killing the messenger bearing the bad news, tell a story of praise. Mike's bad news gave us the chance to correct the problem before <u>all</u> the steam traps were installed.

2. **Customer satisfaction is when the product wears out and the customer is satisfied.**
Armstrong International, Inc. is almost 100 years old and our reputation has been built on quality, service, and trust. Armstrong Service, Inc. will stand for the same thing and live to the ripe old age of 100.

3. **Quality is a continuous journey.**
We have been improving the quality of Armstrong Inverted Bucket Steam Traps for over eighty years. The journey is never over. **NEVER!**

44.

VALENTINES DAY

The sound of a violin could be heard as I approached the building. When I opened the doors, the sweet notes were bouncing off the walls. There in front of me stood a man in a black tuxedo with a red carnation. In his hand was a violin, and I watched as he drew the bow across the strings. Out of the corner of my eye I saw some people watching. I turned and noticed two people I had never seen before leaning against the wall listening. Then my eyes drifted toward the reception desk of Armstrong Service where I saw Donna Sealy and Janette Vazquez listening to the music with smiles on their face. Donna and Janette each held a red rose in their hand. I looked up to the second floor and saw ten or twelve Armstrongers listening as the violinist played his song. Within a few minutes, the song ended and the man took the violin from his chin.

Donna and Janette then turned to me, "Good morning David. We'd like to introduce you to Gail Hines & Joe Bellow from AmeriSuites."

"Good morning Mr. Armstrong."

"Good Morning. You're from the hotel we often use for our seminars and out of town guests, aren't you?"

"Yes, sir. We are very thankful for your business. Come visit us soon."

I started walking to the conference room when I looked back and once again saw the red rose in Donna and

Janette's hands. Then I remembered it was February 14, Valentines Day.

A "Thank you" should be memorable.

THE MORAL OF THE STORY

1. **Most will thank a customer....** but how many will say thank you with a violin?
AmeriSuites was thanking Donna and Janette for sending business to their hotel. AmeriSuites knew whom to serenade for future business.

2. **Getting a new customer is difficult but keeping a customer may be even more difficult.**
AmeriSuites already had most of Armstrong Services business but they wanted to keep it. The red rose, violin, and, let's not forget, Gail and Joe showing up in person to say thank you will help them to do this. This thank you is more memorable because the effort put into it was more than a written thank you.

45.

ED KIRCHNER'S SECRET

One of my favorite stories ends with Ed Kirchner's secret. Ed Kirchner is the foreman for the maintenance department at Armstrong Machine Works. He manages a staff of six men who can fix anything. (Each of these men cost Armstrong $1.2 million. You read right, $1.2 million. To tell you why each maintenance man is paid $1.2 million would be to repeat myself. The story "The $1.2-Million Maintenance Man" has already been told in my first book, Managing By Storying Around). To continue with the story, Ed has a maintenance schedule that he follows, and one day this schedule brought him to the Armstrong Recreation Building. As he was inspecting the air conditioning unit he noticed the thermostat set at 65 degrees. Ed adjusted it back up. He then looked over at the heater. Everything looked in good condition, but he noticed it was running. So he looked at the thermostat and, behold, the thermostat was set at 78 degrees! "What?!" Ed said to himself. "What do these people think they are doing? Obviously someone has come in and thought it was hot and turned the air conditioner thermostat down to 65, and then later someone else came in thinking it was cold and turned the thermostat for the heater up to 78. Neither person ever thought to turn the other unit off." Ed knew the problem would arise again. Ed decided to use the Kirchner secret and fix the problem once and for all.

A secret told is a secret no more.

THE MORAL OF THE STORY

1. **Some things are not what they seem.**
Your first hint to Ed's secret.

2. **Be comfortable with simplistic service.**
Ed's solution is so simple it's brilliant. Remember the best service is simple service. When servicing a customer, always fix the cause of the problem, not the result of the problem. For example, Ed could have locked the thermostats (the result) so nobody could adjust the thermostats. Locking the thermostats was not Ed's secret. Ed fixed the "cause", which was the Armstrongers adjusting the thermostat. You know—human error! So how did Ed keep the Armstrongers from playing with the thermostats? Only Ed and I know —and I can keep a secret. I know the Armstrongers who use the recreation building in the future will have comfortable temperatures thanks to Ed's service call.

STORIES
TO INSPIRE
INNOVATION

CHAPTER 10

46.

TOP SECRET

Come with me to Kauai, Hawaii. The year was 1991. Armstrong International, Inc., Armstrong-Yoshitake, and Armstrong-Hunt were having a convention where new products would be introduced to the sales force. Over 500 people were flown to Hawaii at the expense of Armstrong International. There were so many new products it would take an entire week to introduce all of them.

  A stage sat before the sales force. The convention got under way with the introduction of Humidiclean®, a new product that would revolutionize humidification. Armstrong's Trap Scan® and Trap Alert® were also introduced, giving goose bumps to the salespeople. Many more products were introduced that week. When the end of the week came, a secret new product on stage was covered by a black sheet. The salespeople were going bonkers. They couldn't figure out what the product was. You see, all the other products which had been introduced were supposed to be a secret, but the sales people knew what they were before they were introduced. But this product -- nobody knew what it was. Yours truly sat on the new product that final day and read a story (of course), before unveiling it. When I finished my story, I stood up and ripped off the black sheet, revealing the product to the audience. Thrills and chills went up their spines. It had been the best kept secret at Armstrong International.

STORIES TO INSPIRE INNOVATION **151**

> *Safety first - safety always.*

THE MORAL OF THE STORY

1. **What made this product the best kept secret?**
It took Charlie Reynolds, Manager or Product Engineering, and his department, only five weeks to develop this product from an idea to a finished product. Five weeks is such a short period of time, nobody had time to gossip about it. Few had time to see it. It didn't take six months; it didn't take a year—just five weeks.

2. **The more complex, the poorer the quality and the longer to develop.** *1st law of successful innovation.*
Practice simple innovation. I still believe simple is best, but understand that something always goes wrong, even when you have a simple idea or keep something complex simple. This new product was very simple in the way it functioned, but still things went wrong. However, <u>more</u> things would have gone wrong if Charlie had designed it to be more complex.

3. **Fast failure learned from with quick corrections is the secret to successful innovation.** *2nd law of successful innovation.*
A bad failure is a slow failure. The worst failure is a slow failure without learning something. Be <u>proud</u> of your past failures, but only if you learn something and take quick actions to correct it.

4. **The more innovation we have, the more quality problems we have.** *3rd law of successful innovation.*
The more new products we develop, the <u>more</u> quality problems we will have. There is no way around this. Accept it. Become comfortable with it. This is not to say that we accept poor quality, just that it is impossible to avoid quality problems with new products. We have had a few problems with this new product. With each passing year, we improve the quality. The good news is that we have sold millions of dollars worth, and our customers have a product with which they're happy. Okay, we have a few customers who are not happy, but that will always be so. As customer's we've all bought a product that was new, requiring several factory recalls. I dare say, most of the time we go back and continue to buy from that same company.

5. **Old technology offers better quality at a lower cost and faster prototyping.** *4th law of successful innovation.*
Charlie took one of our existing products, an M series steam trap, and converted it to this new product. The M series steam trap was proven technology that had existed at Armstrong for over 20 years. Charlie needed to design some new internals. Using this old technology helped Charlie speed up the development time by using Armstrong patterns, saving us testing on the vessel design, and assured that we would have quality. With this, we also knew what the costing would be. The only surprise would come from the new technology -- the internals to be used. Guess what? That's where the problems occurred.

6. **Test, test, test.**

Rubbish! Utter nonsense. This will never guarantee that your product will <u>not</u> have quality problems. Remember the 3rd law of successful innovation. I do believe testing is necessary when safety is concerned, but I will never agree that endless testing will guarantee quality. Obviously, in five weeks, we did not have time to complete the testing on this new product, and yes, we've had some quality problems. Do you remember the other products introduced at the convention, which were tested and retested for months? These have had just as many failures, if not <u>more</u> and many are no longer sold today. Anybody remember the plug valve? How about the first Humidiclean®? And then there's the **"Top Secret"** product we introduced in just five weeks -- **the Armstrong Pump Trap**.

47.

MANIFOLDS

It all started with Warren Tase waking up from a sound sleep at 3:00 a.m. Warren had an idea which would reduce the cost for Armstrong Humidifier Manifolds. It was so simple! He couldn't believe it. Why hadn't he thought of this before? Quickly he searched for a pencil and sheet of paper and began sketching his idea.

Later that morning I received a call from Warren.

"David, I didn't get any sleep last night thanks to you!"

"What do you mean?" I asked.

"Yesterday when you assigned me the project to reduce costs on the humidifier manifold, I asked you a simple question. 'When do you need this project completed?' You smiled and said, 'I need it by April 1st.' I shouted, 'April 1st?!'. That's only six weeks away."

"I remember you seemed really concerned. I could see it on your face, Warren."

"Well, at 3:00 in the morning, I woke up with this idea. It is really simple. If you come to my office I will show you my sketches."

"I'll be right there, Warren."

When Warren finished showing me his idea, I shook my head in disbelief. It was so **simple**.

Embrace simplicity.

THE MORAL OF THE STORY

1. **It was so simple!**
Warren's idea is so simple that I don't even want to mention it in this story for fear that competition might copy it. One of the best strategies for great innovation is simplicity. Here's why…

2. **Simple** …innovation reaches our market **faster**.
Warren hit the April Fool's date because he kept his idea simple. His simple idea requires no new machinery, which has <u>long</u> lead times. There will be no delays waiting for tooling and fixtures. Production units available for sale will follow the April Fool's date by just a few months.

3. **Simple** … innovation is simply **less expensive**.
There will be less money spent on machinery, fixtures, and tooling. The raw material will be inexpensive because it is a stock item. No exotic materials here. Warren's time was kept to 6 weeks, which costs less than a group of people working on a project for 6 months.

4. **Simple**…innovation improves **quality**.
The simpler the idea, the better the quality. Warren's new manifold will improve the performance and capacities over the old design.

48.
THE VOTE

Come with me to the Executive Board Room of Armstrong International. At the head of the table sits the President, Gus Armstrong, with four Vice-Presidents, and several department managers seated along the side. The discussion of the day is whether to continue with the development of a new product called Electronic Humidifier Unit (EHU). David Keech, R&D Manager, is very positive and strongly in favor of developing the EHU. David passionately argues for extra monies and time. He's convinced that his engineers can make the product work. Other managers do not take a strong position and so the meeting is going nowhere. Gus decides to call for a vote.

"Who's in favor to continue development of the EHU?"

"no", says the first Vice President,
"no", repeats the second Vice President.
"no."
"no."
"no."
"yes," shouts David Keech
"no."
"no."
"no."
"no."
"no."
"no."

"no."

Finally it's Gus Armstrong's turn to vote - 'no'. The total vote is thirteen to one. Gus Armstrong stands up and says, "We will continue with the development of the EHU. This meeting is adjourned."

> *One man with courage makes a majority.*
> *Andrew Jackson, 7th US President*

THE MORAL OF THE STORY

1. **So why take the vote?**
Thirteen votes were opposed with only one vote in favor of continuing with the EHU development. One might expect the project to be continued if that single vote had been made by the President, Gus Armstrong; but it wasn't. My father approved the EHU because David Keech believed in it. My father wanted to show David how much he believed in him by voiding the "no" votes — even his own "no". It was now David's project, his personal project, and it was up to David, and only David, to succeed.

2. **Act as though it were impossible to fail.**
David truly believed they could succeed. More important than David's belief was his outward passion. When you want something approved, especially in innovation, you must act like a winner, talk like a champion, smell of confidence that you will not fail, so that those who do not believe can gain strength from you and are not afraid to approve time, manpower and money towards your R&D project.

3. **Never follow competition, force competition to follow us.**
Armstrong International had been the inventor of humidification for the industrial market. We had been very successful for many decades, but now competition was entering the market. David Keech and his engineers took our old humidifier line and decided to change it so that once again we would have the newest product for the market. Competition would have to follow us by developing their own EHU.

4. **"Do-it-right-the-first-timers-promote-me-too-products." – Tom Peters.**
Anyone who tries to develop a new product right the first time, will always have a boring product. Nobody wants to buy a "me-too" product. We all are trying to find ways to make our current products different so we can charge a premium price. Exciting new products are seldom accepted by customers because they fear bad quality and require new skills. It may take years before a new exciting product is accepted. Here are a few: Post-its, fax machines, CNN, cellular phones, GPS, televisions, VCRs, automobiles and the computer.

49.

BABY'S FIRST CHRISTMAS!

$\mathcal{I}$ remember when I received a Christmas card with the title <u>Baby's First Christmas!</u> The picture setting was a brick fireplace with red stockings hung on the mantle, and a red poinsettia positioned between six red candles. Sitting in front of the fireplace were the proud parents with their new baby. I knew the family well and was aware of their new baby. They had asked me to be Godfather and I happily agreed. Just a few months prior to Christmas they had sent out the birth announcement. It read:

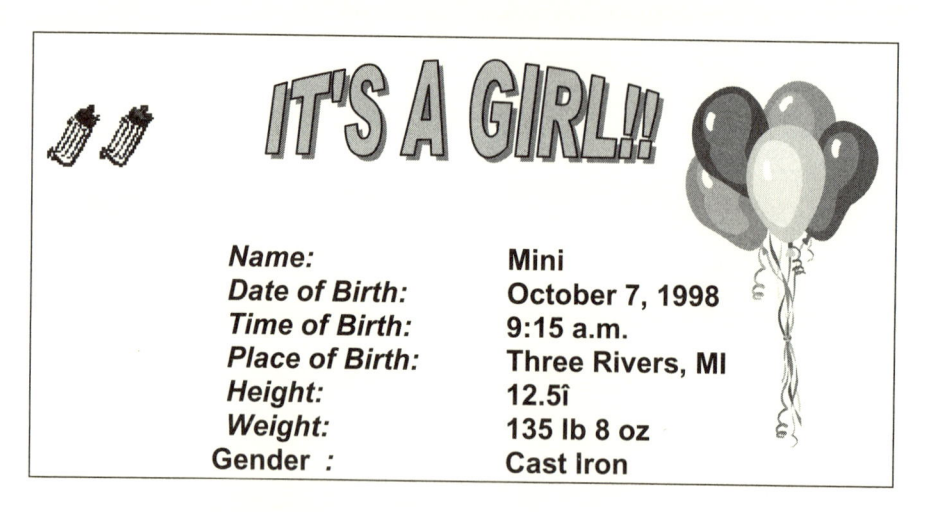

IT'S A GIRL!!

Name:	Mini
Date of Birth:	October 7, 1998
Time of Birth:	9:15 a.m.
Place of Birth:	Three Rivers, MI
Height:	12.5î
Weight:	135 lb 8 oz
Gender :	Cast Iron

You've probably guessed by now that this was a new product announcement. Armstrong Fluid Handling has a line of non-electric pump traps used for lifting hot condensate. A smaller pump trap was needed, which led to the birth of "Mini."

> *Have a cigar!*
> *—Chris Vogel, Armstrong Sales Person*

THE MORAL OF THE STORY

1. **Make new product introductions personal.**
A birth announcement won't get tossed in the wastebasket before it's read. Personal mail has a better chance of being read than business mail. Half the battle is getting your customers and sales force to read their mail. The second half is getting them to remember.

2. **Have A Cigar!**
While Chris Vogel was in the field making sales calls she wrapped the "baby" in a blanket and handed out cigars. What a memorable way to promote a new product.

3. **I want a boy.**
It was Chris who gave birth to this idea. Chris, don't let "Mini" remain an only child for too long.

4. **"Mini" has a birth certificate.**
This birth certificate gave the product's name, height, weight, and material. All the information a customer or engineer would need to know when buying or specifying an Armstrong "Mini" Pump Trap. Once again the birth date was on October 7, 1998.

For you slow learners, it means she became available for delivery on that day.

5. **A good product introduction gets better each time it's told.**

How many times do you think the customer told someone else in their office about this clever mailer promoting an Armstrong Pump Trap?

STORIES TO INSPIRE INNOVATION **163**

STORIES
TO MAKE EVERYONE A **LEADER**

CHAPTER 11

50.

DULL CRAYONS

Believe it or not our crayons have become dull. This happens when people use them to sign in our guest register. The story I'm about to tell you truly happened. It begins at 108 Somogyi Court, South Plainfield, New Jersey. Dick Base was walking through the lobby one day when he noticed that the crayons all had dull tips. He picked up the box of crayons, turned it over, and tried to sharpen a crayon. "Not good enough," Dick thought. He decided to go out and purchase a sharpener so he could sharpen them better. That night he spent quite some time trying to find the perfect sharpener. Eureka! He found one. The next morning Dick sat down in Everlasting Valve's lobby with the box of crayons on his lap and began sharpening. A few crayons later Don Richardson, Sales Coordinator, opened the door to the lobby.

    "Hi, Dick."
    "Good morning, Don."
    "What are you doing?"
    "I'm sharpening crayons. I noticed yesterday that they were really dull, and it was difficult for our guests to sign in with them. So I decided to sit down and sharpen them."
    "That's a good idea. They do look dull."
    Don left and Dick continued sharpening his dull crayons.

Leaders who don't play make boring policies.

THE MORAL OF THE STORY

1. **He who is not willing to have fun is not ready to lead.**
Dick wants everyone to see him sharpening crayons. He sharpens them in the lobby, not behind a closed door. Ah ha! Dick truly believes in having fun.

2. **Leaders will always be vulnerable if they promote having fun at work.**
How many of you are brave enough to sharpen crayons in the lobby for all to see? Cowards! How about calling the Chief Operating Officer, yours truly, and telling this story? Dick did. Dick is my kind of leader.

3. **"A fun leader can't get too far ahead of his followers."**
Are you uncomfortable with the President of Everlasting Valve sharpening crayons? That's right, Dick is the President. Has Dick crossed the line, attempted the unthinkable, lost his marbles? Have you become so complacent, so set in your ways, so boring, unexciting, that you cannot accept the President of a company sharpening crayons? Is Dick really too far ahead of his followers? Maybe just you.

4. **Good leaders tell stories you want to believe in.**
Be honest, don't you want to believe your leaders are just like Dick Base — who like to have fun?

51.

KICK ME!

𝒯his story recounts a time when Grant Kain, Plant Manager of Armstrong Machine Works, was having a bad day. It all started one early morning when Grant was talking with a machinist who had just produced some parts of bad quality.

"How could you run so many pieces of bad quality? Why didn't you catch the first couple of pieces?"

"It's not my fault Grant; we're really busy."

Grant felt his anger growing and quietly he counted to himself 1-2-3-4-5-6-7-8-9-10. Then he spoke. "Remember, you are to practice self-management and inspect your own quality."

"You're right Grant, I'll do a better job next time."

The morning had grown only a few hours older when Grant found himself talking to another machinist about bad quality. "Didn't you see the metal shavings in the casting?"

"No sir, I don't know how I could have missed it, maybe because we're so busy."

Again, Grant could feel his anger growing so he quietly counted to himself 1-2-3-4-5-6-7-8-9-10. "You have time to clean the metal shavings out of a casting! It only takes a minute." Calmly, Grant walked away.

Only a few minutes had passed and, just as Grant was to exit Plant One, a foreman stopped him. "Grant, one of the machinists just crashed one of our dies. The machine is going to be down for at least a couple of days." Grant slowly shook his head then walked away in disgust. As Grant exited the building, he saw a metal bucket and without thinking he gave it a swift kick in anger. The bucket went rattling down the parking lot—clunk, clunk, clunk, clunk.

    The morning was almost over when Grant found himself returning to Plant One. As he approached the door which he had earlier left in anger, he noticed the bucket placed back in its proper place. On the bucket was a happy face with the words ....*kick me*. Grant began to count to himself again 1-2-3-4-5-6-7-8-9-10.

> *"Acting in anger is like putting to sea in a storm."*
> —*Benjamin Franklin*

THE MORAL OF THE STORY

1. **1-2-3-4-5-6-7-8-9-10**.
"When angry, count to ten before taking action; when very angry-100."– Thomas Jefferson. Both Thomas Jefferson and Grant Kain know not to take action when angry. Grant was not angry with the people who put the bucket back making fun of him, but angry with himself. Grant knew that as a leader he should <u>not</u> lose his temper. To keep self-control he would count to ten before speaking. Unfortunately, Grant failed to count to ten and somebody had seen him kick the bucket.

2. **Grant Kain tells the best stories.**
Grant's story ends when he tells me "I left the bucket at the door with the happy face and words *'kick me'* to help remind me to not lose my temper". This bucket has been in the same place outside the tool room door for several years as a constant reminder. Now that you have read this story, all of us, not just leaders, will remember to keep our temper when we see Grant's bucket. You could make decisions for the wrong reasons, such as punishment or to take revenge on another. To read another story that Grant told, look in my first book <u>Managing By Storying Around</u> under the title "Our Promise to Fred Kemp."

3. **Now, what if a subordinate becomes angry?**
If you are the leader let them vent their anger—even towards you. Let them talk, really try and listen to what they are saying. You as the leader must remain calm. If all your efforts fail in calming down your subordinate, then send them home so they have time to think about what they said. The next day the person will normally apologize for their behavior. They are now calm and ready to solve the problem.

52.

EX-PATRIOT

Brian Alfing stood tall. At least it seemed that way from a 6th grader's point of view. We were good friends and spent summers together at baseball camp. I remember Brian telling me one day that he and his family were moving to Belgium. Brian's father had just accepted a new position as General Manager for Armstrong International, Inc. located in Belgium. That following summer, in the year 1970, my parents asked me if I would like to go visit Brian in Belgium. "Of course", I said. I flew to Belgium to stay with Brian and his family for six weeks. I remember how scared I was traveling by myself to Belgium, and how happy I was to see Brian and his father, Norman Alfing, at the airport.

Over 30 years had come and gone since my visit to Belgium. Armstrong International was looking for another ex-patriot to go and live in Beijing, China for two years and work in Kangsen-Armstrong. Kerry Phillips volunteered and was sent. The cold winters with little heat due to government rationing, unfamiliar food, a foreign language, and the hardship of not being near family and friends, reminded Kerry why most people will never volunteer to be an ex-patriot. Kerry knew what other Armstrong ex-patriates like Frank Bowser knew. He looked forward to the adventure of meeting the people, seeing the country and its culture. Kerry also knew the benefits that were to come from Armstrong International.

> *Becoming a leader is not a matter of chance, it is a matter of choice.*

THE MORAL OF THE STORY

1. **Foreign assignments accelerate career advancements.**
This is the reward, the bonus, and the reason to take on a foreign assignment as an ex-patriot. If you want volunteers then you have to provide a benefit. One of the quickest ways to get experience is when you are on your own in a foreign land managing the business. You are the leader. It would be foolish not to use that experience once an employee returns home.

2. **People support what they help create.**
Kerry will be a strong supporter of Kangsen-Armstrong when he is back in the United States. Kerry spent years helping to create a better Kangsen-Armstrong and he won't stop just because he lives in the United States.

53.

ARMSTRONG'S MICHELANGELO

It all started in 1995 while I was walking through Plant Three when a flicker of color caught my eye. Sunlight was beaming through the windows and bright colors were dancing across the shop floor. The bright light and colors drew me towards the assembly department where I found Dan Bronstetter, foreman.

"Who's the Michelangelo?" I asked Dan.

"I am," smiled Dan.

"You painted this floor?"

"I did it on the weekend. Is that OK?"

"Yes, of course! I like the colors, the shapes, and patterns. It reminds me of contemporary art."

"It took me several days to design all the angles, but I like doing it. I started with the area around my desk, and I have hopes to paint more art throughout the assembly department. What do you think?"

"Dan, I like the way the colors brighten up your department. I like the fact that you take pride in your department and want to make it better. I appreciate you doing it on your own time or during slow times, and I am sure the other Armstrongers enjoy it as much as I do. I can't wait to see your next painting on cement canvas."

Leaders adventure too little.

THE MORAL OF THE STORY

1. **Align yourself with leaders who share your vision.**
Dan Bronstetter is a very hard worker and I never thought of Dan as one who likes to play. He is very serious, very demanding, but fair. He builds the best quality and is proud of it. Dan tipped his hand when he started painting the shop floor. Dan likes to have fun.

2. **A leaders most serious activity is play.**
Many leaders will tell you their job is to make a profit; pass valuable information to people who wouldn't have access, yet have a need; provide resources; link compensation to performance; and hire and terminate employees. Few will admit that making work FUN is a priority. I strongly disagree. Our job as leaders is to keep our people from leaving; keep them motivated; keep them creative; and to keep peace among the employees. The best way to do this is to make work fun. I don't mean a little fun, I mean **BIG FUN**!

3. **If a leader's fun isn't big enough, it may go unnoticed.**
Dan Bronstetter is the foreman for the assembly department. He is the leader. What does this leader do? He paints the shop floor bright colors. You can't walk by his department without noticing it. It's big! Dazzling! Outrageous!

4. **Tickets Please.**

You would think you were walking through a museum, not a manufacturing plant. Mike Havens and Harold Coop (see story "Harold Coop, Inc." in this book) have painted their own masterpieces. Others will follow!

54.

ONE HUNDRED DOLLARS

This story begins with Willie Vedmore, Production Control Coordinator, driving to work one morning. It was going to be a nice day. The fog was burning off, the sun had already come up, and there were no clouds in the sky. Willie's eyes were focused on the road when he noticed a car parked on the side of the road. The car was old and in bad shape, and the hood was up, signifying trouble. Standing by the hood was a young mother with her two children. She looked like she was in trouble so Willie decided to pull over to see if he could help.

"Can I help you?"

"I don't know what's wrong. My car won't start! It just stopped when I was driving."

Willie approached the engine, "I don't know much about cars, but let me take a look. Maybe, I can find what's wrong."

While Willie was looking under the hood, Ron Schlesch, Vice-President of Manufacturing for Armstrong, was driving by. Ron saw the young mother who looked like she was in trouble. He decided to pull over to see if he could help.

"Good morning. Can I help you?" asked Ron.

"That's OK. This man is trying to help me."

"Willie, is that you?"

Willie pokes his head out from behind the hood. "Hello Mr. Schlesch, how are you?"

"Just fine. What's the problem?"

"I don't know. She said the car just stopped."

"Let me take a look." Very quickly, Ron decided that the battery had shorted out. Ron reached into his back pocket, pulled out his wallet and gave Willie $100. "Here Willie. Go down to the local auto store and buy her a new battery, then give her the money leftover for gas."

"Ok, Mr. Schlesch."

Ron walked back over to his car, turned around to the young mother and said, "I hope you have a better day." He hopped in the car and drove off to work.

Kindness is greater than any V.P. title.

THE MORAL OF THE STORY

1. **Willie Vedmore never forgot his leader's kindness.**
Willie told us this story 20 years later. Ron probably forgot the story. He may not even know the impact it had on Willie, but Ron gained a strong follower that day. You gain followers <u>anytime</u> and <u>anyplace</u> so be careful what you do or say, even when not at work.

2. **A leader is a dealer in hope.**
Ron gave hope to the mother that things could get better. What started as a car stalled on the road, which would require money for a tow, ended with a new battery and several full tanks of gas.

3. **Do not look for the bad in your boss, look for the good.**
Sometimes your boss makes a decision that is not popular. It is easy to find fault with a boss because every decision has two sides to it and one of those sides always upsets somebody. Willie got a chance to see Ron as a man who cares about others. Willie saw the kindness in Ron. Most people will follow kindness.

55.

YOUR YEARLY PERFORMANCE REVIEW

Have you ever wondered why you didn't get a <u>written</u> review on your performance as an employee? Sure, you get a wage review, and probably a wage increase, and maybe a verbal comment like, "You're doing a good job. Keep it up," but nothing formal or in writing. When I was in my late twenties, I decided to do something about this. I was going to create a very formal written procedure in giving reviews. I spent years going to seminars and creating forms to be used, trying to keep it simple so our managers would want to give the written review. You see, I was convinced our managers didn't give written reviews because they didn't have time, and possibly didn't know how. I even tested my forms on several people in that three-year period. Within a few years we discontinued these written employee evaluations. To find out why, read the morals.

Reviews are better in person than in writing.

THE MORAL OF THE STORY

1. "I don't believe in written employee evaluations," said my father.
"Why?" I asked. Dad answered, "If you have a written review once a year, you are telling your leaders it is okay to

give an employee their evaluation <u>once</u> a year. I think our leaders should do it every day! By not having a written review, we are encouraging our leaders to train, coach, counsel, motivate, or, as you would call it, evaluate their employee each day." Dad was right.

2. **"I've never received my review."**
Shame on you leaders who have someone reporting to you who says this. "But I don't have time," you say. Wrong! You have hundreds of opportunities in a year to give your employees their evaluation. Each day that you talk to your employees (and I know you do because you are practicing Managing By Wandering Around), you can give them some coaching. Dad was right. This is the only fair thing to do with your employees. Constantly give them coaching and guidance. This will be much better and memorable than giving a review once a year.

3. **Sometimes a written review is necessary.**
When an employee is not performing and their job is in jeopardy, you need to put the areas of concern in writing. This is only fair to the employee. It must be crystal clear where he or she must improve.

STORIES
ABOUT FINDING NEW SOURCES OF **PROFIT**

CHAPTER 12

56.

THE DEATH OF A SICK ARMSTRONG PRODUCT

We buried a friend today. A profitable friend who had been with us a long time. The Armstrong Humidimaker was a product developed in the 1960s. It lived a long life, over 30 years, before we killed it and buried it. I remember talking to Armstrong management about putting the Humidimaker out of its misery.

"Gentlemen, do you realize the Humidimaker sales are just over $100,000 per year?"

"Sure, David, but you have to understand we don't take any time promoting it."

"Why is that? Is it because you know we have new products which make it obsolete?"

"Well, that's partly true, but it's still generating over $100,000 in sales."

"I've also noticed that the dollar profits have declined over the last decade. I know that's due to lower sales, but if you look at the profit percent to sales, that has also declined."

"We still make great money, David. The profits are really good when you consider we have almost no selling, general and administrative cost. We spend no advertising dollars, and almost never have to print new literature. The costs are really low; that's why we still sell it."

"I think for the good of the company we need to bury the Humidimaker."

"You can't do that! We have too much inventory. We also have a lot of customers who still like to buy this product. What will they say if we no longer offer the Humidimaker?"

"Why don't you sell them our new, improved EHU unit? I'm sure our customers will understand that we can't continue to carry a line that is not popular. If the customer's complain, offer them a new unit at a reduced price. They'll think Armstrong is doing them a favor. It's time to say good-bye to our old friend. Let's bury it in the next six months."

Sick products require a lot of money.

THE MORAL OF THE STORY

1. **Euthanasia applied to people may be criminal, but not to aging products.**
There is nothing morally wrong with killing this product. The "symptoms" of a sick product are: A sales decline over a period of time; a downward trend in price; declining profit margins; a new product which eliminates the product in question; and too much management time needed to nurse the product to health. This is expensive. Too expensive!

2. **Sometimes there is a cure for the sick product.**
We should look at ideas to reduce costs, change a product feature thus benefit, changing how we advertise, change the market channel, or maybe change the price to make it more

competitive. Burying our products is the last thing we should do.

3. **Once funeral arrangements have been made, you must consider the following.**
Eliminate the confusion and concerns of your customers by offering a substitute product. You will want to carry repair parts for the obsolete product. How long? I recommend for the expected life of the <u>last</u> Humidifier sold. Finally, your inventory must be eliminated efficiently. This is why I gave Armstrong management six months before they were to bury the Humidimaker.

4. **How do we find the sick product?**
You will find a "sick" product where a lot of time and attention are spent yet the sales or profits are poor. Also, look for the <u>new</u> product not being actively promoted with poor sales. You may find our salespeople still promoting the old "sick" product they are comfortable with. We spend large sums of money for the development of new products. We need to get a return on this investment.

57.

$48.45

Are you aware that Armstrong International gave a check for $48.45 to Brady Hooley? This was not for work performed at Armstrong International or reimbursement for travel expenses. Neither, was it a gift. To find out how Brady received his $48.45, you will have to read the story that Kim Lucas, Human Resources Assistant, tells.

It all started with Shelby Hooley going to the Three Rivers Hospital. Later, when Brady received the insurance information in the mail, it looked like the Three Rivers Hospital had been overpaid. Brady (Shelby's father) called the hospital and found out that the Three Rivers Hospital had been overpaid by $242.23. He called Kim Lucas and together they corrected the billing error. After the problem was corrected, Kim Lucas was happy to send a letter and a check for $48.45 to Brady. Kim also honored Brady by telling this story which you've just read.

A fool and his money are soon parted.

THE MORAL OF THE STORY

1. **Reward.....**

> **WANTED**
>
> **Overpaid Medical Bills**
>
> *In 1992, Armstrong International, Inc. added an "Error Incentive Provision" to the health plan. If any employee discovered an error in excess of $100 and succeeded in lowering the bill, he or she would be entitled to 20% of the amount saved, not to exceed $2,000 in a calendar year.*

2. **What gets paid for may not get done . . . believing in the cause is also needed.**
Brady was not aware of the "Error Incentive Provision" to the health plan. Brady went the extra mile to keep our company strong by helping us keep our medical costs down. I hope all Armstrongers believe in keeping our health care program strong, and carefully reviewing their medical bills.

3. **You must believe that the money you spend on medical bills is _your_ money . . . not the company's money.**
Many small companies do not provide health care to their employees. The costs are simply too high. And if they do offer it, it is likely not as good as the Armstrong plan. Check your medical bills for errors. We need more employees like Brady Hooley who practice <u>self-management</u> in keeping costs down on our health insurance. You wouldn't pay a personal bill without looking at it -- would you?

4. **Sniffles, colds, ear aches, sore throats, cuts and bruises.**
The main purpose of any health insurance program is to cover a catastrophe, such as heart attacks, cancer, organ transplants, surgery, etc., which could easily exceed $100,000 per operation, and wipe out your family's savings. Armstrong's health insurance is designed to help protect our employees during these difficult times, not the common cold.

58.

A TREASURE HUNT

The treasure had been hidden for almost 100 hundred years. There had been much talk on how to find and retrieve it. It was not a king's fortune, but it was enough to make one comfortable for the rest of their life. In the year 1998, Dan Torrans, lab technician at Armstrong International, knew where the treasure was, but he needed money and equipment to recover it. For financial support he approached Jim Daugherty, the manager of the Armstrong Lab (commonly referred to as *Tests-Я-Us*. Jim believed in Dan, and purchased the equipment required to recover the treasure.

Armed with the latest technology, manpower and materials, Dan began his treasure hunt. Using an Armstrong pump trap and galvanized pipefittings, he began building a condensate return system that would bring him his treasure. The Cleaver-Brooks and Johnson boilers located in Armstrong's lab were the source of this hidden treasure. Armstrong continuously ran their boilers performing tests on a variety of new products. The boilers were dumping their hot condensate (water) to the ground during each test. Dan knew that if he could return this hot condensate to the boilers he would save Armstrong International the energy used to heat cold water. Dan installed a condensate return system. Shortly thereafter, Armstrong International received its utility bill and found that is had been reduced thanks to this condensate return system. Dan succeeded in finding his treasure that day—energy savings for Armstrong.

Steam marks the spot!

THE MORAL OF THE STORY

1. **Do you have a hidden treasure....A steam system?**
Do you have a treasure map? Armstrong Service in Orlando has steam experts who can provide you with a treasure map. Dan picked up one of those treasure maps and has saved Armstrong International a great deal of money. We would be happy to share with others the knowledge we have on how to save energy while using steam, and which products can make it possible.

2. **What will you find when you open your steam system treasure chest?**
You will find that the condensate needs no softening (it already is), a reduction in the amount of water purchased from the city, no boiler chemicals (because returned condensate has already been treated with chemicals), and, the biggest jewel, **ENERGY SAVINGS!**

3. **You can navigate through the dangerous seas of bureaucracy**.
Dan Torrans and Jim Daugherty found a way, despite company bureaucracy and capital spending limits. Resources and approval can be found if you only look, but it takes the heart of a pirate on a treasure hunt to succeed.

59.
CAMELOT

Ride with me to Camelot where we find the knights of Armstrong Service sitting at the round table. The king asked what perils threatened the kingdom. Sir Gibson stood up and placed 100 gold coins in the center of the table. Sir Gibson was also the keeper of the kingdoms treasure.

"I place these gold coins in front of my king to remind him that for every minute we sit at the round table, the kingdom spends 100 gold coins."

"Are ye sure?" Asked the King.

"Quite sure."

"That would mean for 60 minutes, the cost to the kingdom is 6000 gold coins and an 8 hour day would cost 48,000 gold coins."

"My point exactly," answered Sir Gibson.

Sir Kealy handed out scrolls showing what costs could be eliminated. "We must be careful how many guards we have at the Palace. We must first be sure that we have a war to fight before we recruit soldiers."

"I agree, but it is difficult to know when a war will begin. We must have some soldiers in advance so we are prepared." Sir Fonner replied.

Sir Quirin leaned forward and said, "And the recruits, these would-be soldiers, must have fought in many wars and have experience. We cannot hire mere farmers and young boys, for we will surely lose the battle."

"Do we have allies who need our support?" asked the King.

Sir Bloss spoke quickly, "Yes, our ally, the Heinz Kingdom is in need of our help. They need men, supplies and our knowledge on how to fight a war against steam breathing dragons."

> *Time is money.*
> *--Ben Franklin*

THE MORAL OF THE STORY

1. **Put your money on the table.**
The 100 gold coins that Steve Gibson placed on the table was really a Ben Franklin $100 bill. Steve placed this $100 bill on the round table before the meeting began. The purpose of the meeting was to help control expenses at Armstrong Service and to plan for future cash needs. Armstrong Service was a start-up company and over the past few years had consumed a lot of cash. To show just how much cash, Steve Gibson explained to the management (the knights) how much each minute costs. Every time a discussion centered on spending money, the $100 bill was before us on the round table to remind us how much we were spending. Steve's creativity truly helped keep us focused on the purpose of the meeting, which was to control expenses, control cash flow, and make sure our future projects were profitable. Steve had been explaining expense concerns for quite sometime in the financial package but the $100 bill brought it to <u>life</u>.

2. **Heinz is our ally.**

Heinz and Armstrong Service had just entered into an agreement. Armstrong will help supply Heinz steam needs for making ketchup and soup. Yes, Heinz also makes soup. Certain assets of Heinz will be purchased by Armstrong, which will require cash payment.

3. **The story of King Arthur.**

This story takes place at Armstrong Service in Orlando, Florida in a conference room called – Camelot. There is a round table in this room, which looks like the round table found in the story of King Arthur. King Armstrong and his knights became aware of the kingdom's expenses that day. Sir Gibson had done his job as treasurer.

60.

LET THERE BE LIGHT

"Hey, Joyce. Ya got a minute?" Keith Pratt flagged down Joyce Clay, the Manufacturing Resource Officer, as she walked through the machine shop.

"Sure, Keith. What's up?"

"Well, I've got a problem. Since we moved the new Magnum machine in, we don't have adequate lighting here." Keith took Joyce to the back of the machine where the tooling control panel was located.

"See how dark it is? I have to use a flashlight to check this panel and make adjustments with one hand."

"It slows you down and jeopardizes accuracy doesn't it?" Joyce asked.

"Exactly. Now follow me to the Maxum machine." Keith motions with his hand. "We need a bench and better lighting here also. Dennis Cuttler in the tool room has noticed that we don't always use all four corners on the inserts. Sometimes we miss two or even three corners. We can't see well enough to know if the corner is worn so we just put in a new one."

"But Keith, that increases the cost of our tooling by 50%-75%. If that insert has four sides and you only use one side and the cost of the tooling is $100.00, then you've wasted $75.00. We can't do that."

"I know, I know, but nobody will listen to me."

"Have you talked to your foreman?"

"Yes."

"Have you talked to maintenance?"

"Yes."

"Have you talked to the Plant Manager?"

"Yes, but they all have bigger problems."

"Raising the cost of tooling 75% is a big problem, Keith. Let me see what I can do."

Joyce went back to her office and pulled up the cost of several inserts, checked the piece rate per corner, extrapolated the increased cost, and then went to see Dan Findlay.

"Hey Dan, can I have five minutes of your time?" Joyce presented her case, and Dan readily agreed. The next day Keith not only had adequate lighting on both machines, but a bench to examine his inserts.

> *Many receive advice, few profit by it.*
> *Publilus-Roman Writer*

THE MORAL OF THE STORY

1. **Waste not, want not.**
In this story, the operators were throwing away tooling that still had two or three sharp edges to cut with. Keith saw the problem and found the answer. Joyce Clay heard Keith's advice and took action. Joyce was quick to point out that not wasting this expensive tooling would help justify the investment for proper lighting. Seems obvious to me, but I'll say it anyway. Look for waste to save money. Profound—don't you agree?

2. **Nine-tenths of reducing cost is being wise in time.**
Joyce could have waited weeks, even months, but she took action that very same day. Every day she saved by taking quick action improved the profits that much more.

61.
SCRAP

I was a young man just out of college. Yvonne and I had just purchased our first home. We lived in an area where thunderstorms were very common. The lightening from these storms could create serious problems with our television set. Wanting to protect it, I asked for advice from a fellow Armstronger.

"You need to ground your house, David."

"How do I do that?"

"Find some heavy gauge wire, attach it to a lighting rod, and then secure it to something in the ground that will conduct electricity."

"What would that be?"

"Oh there's a lot of things you could use. Why don't you see if there is some bar stock, preferably brass, in the scrap bin and use that? You're working in the spindle department, right?"

"Yeah, I've been there for one week."

"There's a big scrap rack in that department full of bar stock. I'm sure you can find what you need there."

Sure enough, he was right. The next day I found a nice piece of brass bar stock about 1½" in diameter and 3-feet in length. With it tucked tightly underneath my arm, I began to leave the factory after my shift. I got no more than 30 steps out the door when Bob Scott, General Foreman saw me and asked me what I was doing.

"Oh I found this great piece of bar stock, Bob, and thought I'd use it to ground out my house in case it gets struck by lightening."

"That's a good idea, David, but do you know how much that bar stock is worth?"

"Nothing - it's scrap."

"Try $50." Replied Bob. "We sell our scrap"

"How much?"

"I'm guessing David, but I would assume $40-$50. You should go to accounting and let them know you are taking it so you can pay back the company."

Forty dollars was more than I wanted to spend so I returned the bar stock with a new lesson learned.

Even scrap has value

THE MORAL TO THE STORY

1. **Scrap is like promises-easier made than kept**.
We always look to reduce the amount of scrap we produce. We should tell our new employees that scrap has value. We may not be able to eliminate scrap, but we can definitely eliminate missing scrap by educating our employees about its value.

2. **What's better than scrap - No scrap**.
As a reminder, scrap is always welcome instead of poor quality hidden and passed onto our customers.

62.

TOMORROW IS NOT PROMISED

I remember the last time I saw Mike Furey at his workbench. He had just shaved his head due to chemotherapy treatments, but he had a big smile on his face. He was still working as hard as ever, and producing great quality products. When I shook his hand, it wasn't as strong as usual. I knew the cancer was taking his strength. We talked for several minutes about his battle against cancer. I gave him some words of encouragement and told him stories about people who had survived this dreaded disease. Mike smiled and said he remembered some of the people. I told Mike our prayers are with him.

I then walked back to my office. Later it was brought to my attention that even with the chemotherapy treatments, Mike had only missed a few days of work. Most people would have missed several weeks. This didn't surprise me, for Mike was always one of our best employees in regard to work habits. Shortly after my visit, Mike passed away leaving his wife Sharon and three children, Benjamin, Joshua and Jamie Lynn.

A good wife and health is a man's best wealth.

THE MORAL OF THE STORY

1. **'In a word where the bottom line is so often money, Armstrong's bottom line is compassion.'**
This excerpt appeared in a letter that was printed in the Three Rivers Press newspaper when Mike's sister, Marcia Post, wrote this letter to the editor.

2. **A good reputation is a company's greatest asset.**
Sharon sent me a letter a month and a half after the death of Mike, giving praise and thanks to Armstrong for its compassion and financial support. Instead of calling Sharon or writing a letter, I wrote this story about her husband to remind her how much he touched our lives at Armstrong International.

Stories

About Why **Small** Is Beautiful

63.
THE $55,000 COMB

This story has been told all too often. A friend of mine, Greg Welch, had just taken a new job with Nabisco Company. The new job required Greg to relocate from New York to Chicago. While looking for a house, he decided to rent an apartment near the office. During the first week Greg felt it important to meet all the people who would be working with him. A meeting was scheduled in a hotel so that afterwards everyone could spend the evening together. Greg wanted to spend as much time as possible with everyone, and at the last moment decided to spend the night at the hotel, even though his apartment was nearby.

The next morning, after Greg finished his shower, he realized he had forgotten his comb. He knew he had a meeting at 8:00 a.m., so he called the front desk.

"This is Greg Welch in Room 143. Could you have someone bring a comb to my room? I forgot mine."

"I'm sorry Mr. Welch. We don't have any combs here at the front desk, and the hotel store is closed until 9:00 a.m."

"That's too late. My meeting starts at 8:00 a.m., and I need one now. You know, I'm spending $55,000 with your hotel this week. Can't you find me a comb?"

"Sir, I don't know what to do. I'm sorry . . . ah, we just don't have any combs."

Greg finished getting dressed, hopped in his car, drove to the local store down the block, and bought a comb for 59-cents.

The little things count.

THE MORAL OF THE STORY

1. **It's only a comb!**
That may be so, but that is all Greg talked about when he told me his story. He didn't tell me how nice the rooms were, how good the service was, or how great the food tasted. He talked about a 59-cent comb. Is Greg being unfair to the hotel and the people behind the front desk when he tells this story? Let's be honest. We have all gotten upset, maybe even angry, about a little thing that has inconvenienced us at some time in our life. Why is that? I believe we all expect to get a "no" answer, or "I can't help you" when our demands are expensive, dangerous, complicated, or unfair. In most cases, however, the little things never involve these conditions. A comb is not dangerous, expensive, unfair or complex, so we expect to hear "Yes, I can help you." Is it fair that Greg was unhappy because of a 59-cent comb? I think so. Don't let it happen at Armstrong International.

64.

PEWWWW!

It is a hot, muggy day in the middle of summer. Two large twelve-foot doors are wide open, but no breeze can be felt in the factory. Perry Wright, machinist on the Cincinnati Milacron, is just starting his shift. He approaches his machine and slides the doors open.

"Pewwwwwww!!" It smells like rotten eggs, and Perry almost passes out. "I hate this new coolant we are using. Every time it gets hot, it stinks." Quickly he closes the doors and goes to find Grant Kain.

"Grant, would you follow me over to the Cincinnati machine? I want you to smell the new coolant on a hot summer day."

"Sure, let's go." Grant approaches the machine and as he opens the doors, his eyes water and he turns his head gasping for fresh air. Quickly shutting the doors he turns to Perry and says, "Pewwww! Pump this coolant out of the machine, and put the <u>old</u> coolant back in. I don't care how much extra life we get out of our tooling and machinery by using the new coolant. Nobody can work with that kind of smell."

Nothing is too small to fix.

THE MORAL OF THE STORY

1. **Armstrong leaders care about small things.**
By using the smelly new coolant, Armstrong could extend the life of its tooling and machines. This could save Armstrong a lot of money. Grant knew not to put money ahead of our employees, even if it's a small thing like *smell*. If you are a leader and don't care about small things, you don't deserve your title.

2. **Perhaps the most critical element of decision making is timing.**
Perry knew the time was now. The smell was at its worst. Grant would surely smell this **little** problem once he opened the doors.

3. **Is this smelly story too small of an issue to tell the Chief Operating Officer?**
I don't think so, and neither does Perry who stopped me while I walked through the factory. Perry was happy to praise Grant for taking action in this story. Perry told me this story.

4. **Did it bother you**......that I used Chief Operating Officer instead of Chief Storytelling Officer?
Good! Just one little word can make all the difference.

65.

THE APRON

When you hear this story you may not believe it's true, but it is. It all started with Edna Hoffman busy at her sewing machine. She pulled the dark blue cloth through the machine. The needle moved quickly as it sewed letter after letter on the apron. Finally, the last stitch had been made and Edna leaned back and looked at her work with pride. It was ready for delivery.

The apron next appeared on my desk. As I unfolded it, I read the words 'Harold Coop, Inc." Pinned to the apron was a note: "I thought you would like to deliver this to Harold Coop. Yours truly, Edna Hoffman". There was no way I was going to deliver this to Harold Coop. I picked up the apron and walked over to Edna's desk.

"Edna, I am not delivering this apron to Harold. **We** are going to deliver this apron to Harold."

It's the small company culture we seek.

THE MORAL OF THE STORY

1. **Do you remember Harold's story?**
Refer to my story "Harold Coop, Inc." Edna Hoffman remembers this story. That's why she made the apron. The short version of this story was that Harold Coop

worked in Armstrong's factory. Harold wanted to be a soleproprietor so one week he painted his equipment and added the Armstrong Logo to his machines. Harold's pride made you believe he owned his own business. Edna thought Harold should dress the part of an owner. The apron with his company's name on it was just the small finishing touch to make the apron perfect.

2. **I am not sure if big companies can appreciate what you do as an employee.**
I do know that small companies can. So if you want to know if your company is too big, answer these following questions:
- **Have you ever met the person who signs your paycheck?** If you haven't, your company is probably too big.
- **Have you met the person who is at the top of your organization?** If not, your company is probably too big.
- **Do you have assigned parking spaces?** If you do, you are too big. I don't think Harold has an assigned parking spot.
- **Do you know everyone's name in your company?** If you don't, you're too big.
- **Do you know all the fax numbers, phone numbers, 800 numbers to your company?** If not, you're too big.
- **Do you have a thick policy manual?** If yes, you're too BIG!!
- **Do you use last names at work.** If yes, you're too big.

66.
WHO PARKED IN MY PARKING SPACE?

Knock Knock!! I look up from behind my desk and see Kim Lucas at my office door. "Come in, Kim."

"David, did you drive the green Lincoln Towncar today?"

"Ahhhhhhhhhhh, yes, I did."

"Did you park it out front near the sign that says 'Reserved'?"

"I might have, why is somebody complaining that I took their parking spot?"

"No."

"You know, Kim, I really have a problem with assigned parking spots. We don't have job descriptions, we don't use last names, we don't have hierarchy charts; why would we have parking spots designated for employees?"

"Nobody complained David, I just thought you would like to know that the spot you took was reserved for your grandfather."

"My grandfather! Why didn't you tell me?" I jumped out of my chair, grabbed my keys, and went out to move the car.

Assigned parking spots means our company is too big.

THE MORAL OF THE STORY

1. **Assigned parking spots means a slow decision—making company.**
If a company takes time to assign employees parking spots, it has too many rules and policies. Companies with too many rules and policies have more excuses for bureaucracy. More bureaucracy means slow decision making. That's Death!

2. **A big company falls into the trap of managing its size instead of using it.**
As a company grows its number of employees grow causing a parking problem. Management assigns parking spots so they get a spot—a *good* spot. Why not allow open parking so the first employees who show up at work can choose their spot? Shouldn't we reward the hard working employees? If you're wondering, do I practice what my morals preach? The answer is yes. Kathy Spencer, my assistant, took my favorite parking spot her third day on the job because she comes in to work before I do.

3. **Small companies give people voice.**
Kim knows me well enough to ask me to move my car. Kim knows me because we don't have layers of hierarchy, because we use first names, because my door is open, and because we act like a small company.

4. **Bureaucracy starts quietly with your first policy...**first assigned parking spot.
When does it stop? Soon nobody will do anything unless it's covered by a policy. My grandfather had an assigned parking spot near the door because he was 89 years old.

5. **I allow assigned parking spots for two reasons.** The first is to reward those employees for their loyalty in staying with Armstrong. The second is because Tom Grubka, General Manager, once gave up his parking spot near the front door to a pregnant employee during the winter months. Tom parked across the street for many months.

STORIES
TO INSPIRE
SELF-MANAGEMENT

CHAPTER 14

67.
IOU'S

Have you heard the story about Armstrong's IOUs? You can find them in the cafeterias. If you read my story, "The Cafeteria," in <u>Managing By Storying Around</u>, you will recall that Armstrongers pay for the food they select on the *honor* system. There is a cash register, but the door is open and full of money for making change. Nobody is there to make sure that the Armstrongers pay. There are occasions when an Armstronger has no money, or cannot make change for a large bill. For these occasions there is a notepad by the cash register where they sign their name and the amount of money owed. They are to pay this off at the end of the week, which should be possible since payday is Friday. If they don't pay it off, an IOU is created.

The IOUs have been stacking up lately, and it's becoming a concern of ARMSTAG (a company club managed by employees). People simply are not paying off their IOUs. It's gotten so bad that Tom Grubka, General Manager, was asked to hand-deliver several of the IOUs in hopes of improving collections. Some Armstrongers got the message and paid off their IOUs, but there are still many who have not. Read the morals to find out how we are going to deal with those Armstrongers who don't pay off their IOUs.

STORIES TO INSPIRE SELF-MANAGEMENT

You should be ashamed of yourself!

THE MORAL OF THE STORY

1. **The shame of an IOU.**
It used to be embarrassing if you had an IOU. People were ashamed because they did not pay off their bill at the end of the week. There was no pride in having an IOU in your pocket. Due to this shame and loss of pride, we had very few IOUs. Not paying off your IOUs will not become an Armstrong tradition. This is one tradition we don't need.

2. **Do away with the IOUs?**
No! If we do away with the IOUs, Armstrongers could forget to pay their bills. There are those days when Armstrongers do not have the exact change, or any money with them, and yet are hungry. They will take the food, saying to themselves, "I will pay tomorrow, " and then honestly forget to pay, without a reminder. That's where an IOU comes in. IOUs were meant to be a reminder, not a loan. Stop using the IOUs as loans!

3. **Do away with the honor system in our cafeterias?**
Again, the answer is no. I ask all Armstrongers to help ARMSTAG collect on these IOUs, just as each of you help co-workers come to work on time by hitting hammers on workbenches to make lots of noise when someone is late.

4. **IOUs must support the tradition of honesty at Armstrong International.**
Some will argue that their IOU is for a small amount of money, and it doesn't matter. Wrong! Armstrong's honor system, where we trust each other, lies one step from

extinction when somebody takes advantage of it. Unpaid IOUs, no matter how small, do just that.

68.

NEXT DAY DELIVERY

*J*ust the other day I was walking through Plant Three when Gary Blood, in shipping, signaled me to come and talk to him. I quickly turned down the aisle and approached him as he finished putting a label on a package.

"You need me, Gary?"

"Yes David, I'm confused. I was reading your book last night, and one of the stories about partnerships got me thinking. The title of the story was "Nice Guys Finish First," and one of the morals to this story talked about the importance of reducing the price to a customer <u>before</u> they ask for a price reduction. Do you remember this story?"

"Yes," I replied. "The titles help me remember what each story is."

"Well here is where I am confused. Sometimes a customer wants us to ship their product so it arrives the next day. This requires air-freight. I am supposed to use UPS, but sometimes I use Emery Worldwide because the cost is almost half. I think it's because Emery Worldwide charges by weight while UPS charges by cubic feet. Since our humidifiers don't weigh much, but take up a lot of space, it is normally cheaper to ship by Emery Worldwide. Many times I change the shipping instructions to save the customer money. I check with the customer before doing this. If we ship by UPS Armstrong receives a rebate based on volume shipped. Now here is my question: If we ship by Emery Worldwide, we reduce UPS shipments. If we reduce UPS shipments, we reduce profits for Armstrong but we save the customer money. Am I doing the right thing?"

"Yes. The stories support what you are doing."

"I thought I was doing the right thing. We always talk about reducing cost in the product, but we can also reduce the cost to the customer by shipping the product cheaper. I always try to write a little note sending it with the product. It tells the customer I changed to Emery Worldwide to save them money."

> *We are all in this alone.*
> —*Lily Tomlin-comedian*

THE MORAL OF THE STORY

1. **We are all in this alone.**
Many of you are alone throughout the day when you have a chance to improve the success of Armstrong. Gary found himself alone when he came to the decision to save the customer money on its freight. He made a decision...would you?

2. **He who does nothing, need hope for nothing.**
If Gary had done nothing, then he need not hope for a production bonus, a salary, health benefits, vacation, a year end bonus, a pension, etc...

3. **It's not my job.**
Be careful...you may talk yourself out of work if you believe this, and eventually out of your job. Gary could have said,

"It's not my job to find a cheaper way to ship the product," but he knew that this could result in losing future orders because the total cost to the customer would be higher than competition. All of our jobs depend on keeping our customers happy. The best way to do this is to treat every job as if it was your job.

69.

DIRECTOR OF FIRST IMPRESSIONS

This story begins with an Armstrong Employee returning home after a *fun* day at work.

"Hi Honey! Grab your coat, we are going out to dinner to celebrate."

"Celebrate what?"

"I got my promotion today. It took me 20 years at Armstrong but I did it."

"Wow, I'm so proud of you. You've worked so hard. When does the new promotion go into effect?"

"Tomorrow. I can hardly wait to go to work."

The new day came and with pride the Armstronger took the nametag, which said 'Director of First Impressions', and placed it carefully on the wooden desk. Diane Reece sat down and before she could get comfortable her first visitor came in.

"Excuse me. I am here to see Sue Boele in purchasing."

"I'll let her know you're here. While you wait, would you please sign our register and don't forget to use our crayon," noted Diane.

"Sue said she is going to be a few minutes. You may want to grab one of David Armstrong's books of stories about Armstrong International. If you wish, I can turn on the television so that you can watch some *video stories* (over the Armstrong Television Network) about our Company."

Only believe.

THE MORAL OF THE STORY

1. **Only believe…**without any doubt that you are a Director, with all the power and respect that comes with the title.
Empower yourself! You are Diane Reece, Inc. Gary Ford believes that the receptionist should have a title befitting her responsibilities, so Gary awarded her the title, "Director of First Impressions."

2. **To believe in self management without good works…**is a **false** belief.
Diane promotes the use of the crayons. She encourages the television to be turned on, she offers our books of stories to be read, she brews the gourmet coffee, she answers the phone quickly and tries to make "her" guests comfortable. That's the key. **Her** guests, not Armstrong International's guests. The title "Director of First Impressions" means nothing if you are not willing to do the work of a Director.

3. **A company is known by its receptionist…** or should I say "Director of First Impressions."
Who is probably the first person our customers, vendors, partners, potential hires, etc. meet when they come through the doors to Armstrong? Diane Reece, our "Director of First Impressions." It is, therefore, very important that Diane

prepares our guests for what will be a unique experience at Armstrong.

4. **We need more Directors of First Impressions.**
So, we made several nameplates for all the receptionists of each Armstrong Division. To make sure each receptionist understood the title, we sent this story with each nameplate.

70.

THE CHAUFFER

"Home, James". The company car slowly pulls out of the parking lot of Kangsen-Armstrong. Kerry Phillips sits quietly in the backseat looking out the window at the sights of China. He had been living in China for almost two years and still enjoyed looking at the sights. The silence was broken as James spoke.

"Zhou guai"

"Yes, left turn", Kerry repeats. The car stops in front of the Swissotel. Kerry says "Ming tian jin?"

"See you tomorrow," repeats James.

The Next Day...........

Another fun day of work and Kerry was ready to go home to his hotel in Beijing. As he came out of the doors of Kangsen Armstrong, he approached James at the company car. "I'm ready to go home."

"Just a few more minutes, I am not done cleaning the car."

Kerry quietly waited as James continued to clean the car. This was not the first time. Within a few minutes, Kerry was on his way home, once again gazing out the window looking for new sights.

James Yang Limousine Company.

THE MORAL OF THE STORY

1. **James Yang Limousine Company.**
We want our employees to think like entrepreneurs. James treats the <u>company</u> car as if it were his own personal cab/limousine. If our employees believe they are independent businesses, they will manage themselves. Remember my story, "Director of First Impressions."

2. **Home James.**
Would you be mad if your chauffer was not ready to leave when you were? Kerry was not angry as he told me this story. He was proud of James. Kerry could not complain and demand to leave because he wanted to keep the entrepreneurship spirit alive in James. Small companies are more focused on what they do, are streamlined; and, are risk takers. James was focused on keeping his car clean. Would he have cared about the dirt if it were only a company car? I think not.

3. **Large divisions can spin off small companies.**
Why stop there? Why not spin off a new company centered around one machine, one department or one company car?

71.

ARMSTRONG'S GENERAL STORE

𝓑UZZZZZZZZZZZZ went the alarm clock waking up Lori Samson and Pat Reed. Each of the Armstrongers were half asleep as they look at their alarm clocks—**5:30 a.m.** Just enough time to get ready and drive to Kmart and be one of the first customers waiting for the doors to open for the Christmas discounts. Lori and Pat had some shopping to do for their family and the Armstrong General Store. Lori and Pat had decided to help decorate the store by finding fabrics, Christmas decorations and other items which would help give it the illusion of being an early 1900's General Store. When they exited Kmart with bags in hand, they still were missing some items. They decided to go south to Shipshewana, Indiana and shop in some antique stores. They were not going to give up on their hunt for early 20th century relics! The trip to Shipshewana turned out to be a big success. That Saturday afternoon they returned to Armstrong International and papered the walls, repainted the floor, and decorated the General Store.

    Several days later, the sign hanging on the front door said--**Open**. Immediately, some customers found their way to the General Store to do some shopping. Several employees throughout the day had also visited the Armstrong General Store to place their orders for the Christmas holidays. Everyone noticed how authentic the Armstrong General Store looked. You really felt like you were stepping back in time. Lori and Pat had done a great job. The only thing that seemed to be missing was a black pot-bellied stove. Other Armstrongers soon caught the desire to help make the Armstrong General Store look even more authentic. Edna Hoffman made a scarecrow with a ceramic smiling face that welcomes visitors to the Armstrong General Store and Joyce Clay placed bolts of calico fabric on the shelves. The General Store was open for business, but where was the store clerk?

Self-Management gets better with practice.

THE MORAL OF THE STORY

1. **Who needs a store clerk?**
Remember, the General Store is located inside the Armstrong factory where Armstrong employees are <u>trusted</u>. Armstrong Café has no person operating the cash register, and neither will Armstrong's General Store. We don't want Armstrongers to think that we no longer trust them by having a store clerk. Yes, somebody could steal merchandise, but they won't. Besides, you never know when a fellow co-worker might be watching.

2. **Where is the black pot-bellied stove?**
Lori and Pat could have purchased a black pot-bellied stove, but they didn't. It was more money than they wanted to spend and maybe if they waited they would find one that was cheaper. They were spending the company money as if it was their own—very cautiously.

3. **BUZZZZZZZZZZZZZ.**
Lori and Pat woke up at 5:30 in the morning so they could get the best discount. Let us also remember they gave up their Saturday (their own personal time), for the benefit of their fellow employees.

4. **On Sale.**
There will be no signs marked 'sale' because all items are sold at cost. One of the benefits for selling at cost is that our employees are able to save money. A second benefit is to run the store simply. We will not have to collect sales tax since there is no profit.

5. **Do you have my size?**
We actually keep one size of every item in stock and we have a clothes rack with each of the sizes on it so people can try on the shirts and sweatshirts to make sure they select the right size. When they fill out their order form they will also leave a check for payment. The following Tuesday their merchandise will arrive and can be picked up in the General Store at their convenience.

6. **Hidden benefits from the Armstrong General Store.**
We like to give our guests who attend our product steam seminars free gifts. During the plant tour we also stop by the Armstrong General Store where they can purchase something else. Most of the items carry the Armstrong logo and name. When our guests, or shall I say customers, return to their company, they will be advertising our company as they walk around wearing their new Armstrong hat or shirt. Or maybe while they are writing a purchase order they will see the Armstrong logo on their Cross pen and remember to give Armstrong some business.

7. **Employee Pride.**

Our employees will be seen in town wearing the Armstrong logo.

8. **Armstrong Characters.**

We could use the General Store as another excuse to have an Armstrong character. We need a store entrepreneur or store manager, don't we? Perhaps, when we have our college students come back to work during the summer or Christmas, they can manage the store and get first hand experience on what it is like to take orders, deliver the orders, and deal with customer complaints. For more information on this, refer to my story "Armstrong Scholarship Program" found in my book, <u>Managing by Storying Around</u> and turn to the story "Armstrong Cleaners, Inc." found in this book.

STORIES ABOUT **STORYTELLING**

CHAPTER 15

72.

ARMSTRONG'S FIRST HONORARY EMPLOYEE

Have you heard the story Janel Atwood tells about Doug Cribbs? Both of these people work at Eagle Alloy, a partner of Armstrong International. Janel's story begins with an Armstrong part C-1146-A. Many of the Eagle employees are familiar with this part. They are familiar because it is a difficult part to work with and has required many engineering and pattern changes to get it where it is acceptable to Armstrong International. Even after all these changes have been made, the part Eagle Alloy works on still requires special care. How much care? With Eagle Alloys' scrap rate ranging between 20-30% on this part, it requires a lot of attention. This is way above Eagle Alloy's goal of 2.4 %, and even higher than their typical scrap rate.

Jeff Cook of the sales department started looking at the production information from employees on the floor to see where he could help make improvements. What Jeff found is that when Doug Cribbs made these parts, the scrap rate fell from 20-30% down to 3%. It was an amazing difference. So what was Doug's secret? "Ownership of the job," says Jeff. "Doug is conscientious when putting the core together, he takes a few extra minutes to handle it carefully and that shows in the quality of the end product." Armstrong International notices quality too. Marcia Kaup, Purchasing Manager at Armstrong International, wanted to do something special for Doug. So Marcia made a trip to

Eagle Alloy with some special gifts for Doug. Among them was a certificate of appreciation from Armstrong International naming Doug an honorary employee.

Stories create role models.

THE MORAL OF THE STORY

1. **Stories are for a thousand ears to hear.**
Janel Atwood wrote this story about Doug Cribbs in Eagle Alloy's employee newsletter. Janel brought it to life for all Eagle Alloy employees. Marcia Kaup re-told this story at Armstrong International. May all employees learn from this story.

73.
A VOICE FROM THE PAST

Twenty years ago a girl eight years old was hit by a car and needed surgery. Her mom and dad knew what they had to do, but the surgery was very expensive. Like any mother or father, they humbled themselves for the sake of their little girl and asked for help. Roger Closset, at that time the Plant Manager of Armstrong International Belgium, heard their plea for help. Roger began asking others in the community for donations. He approached the Armstrong employees for their contributions.

"It was amazing!" said Roger. "You would find Armstrong employees at the soccer field collecting money during half-time, sponsoring fundraisers, and digging in their pockets so that this little girl could afford her surgery and hospital stay."

Just a short while ago, Raymond Barrett, Financial Controller for Armstrong Belgium, found himself in need of a temporary assistant. His current assistant was taking maternity leave. Armstrong International began searching for a temporary assistant. Elvia Montanini applied for the job. Elvia got the temporary job even though her voice sounded a little different than yours and mine, the result of surgery years before. Soon thereafter, Raymond's assistant came back from maternity leave. Elvia approached Roger and said that she would be interested in a full-time job at Armstrong. Everybody had been very pleased with Elvia so they hired her August 10, 1998.

One night Roger was working late when the cleaning lady came by.

"So I see you've hired Elvia. She's one of my neighbors."

"Really?" said Roger.

The cleaning lady continued, "It was really nice of Armstrong to hire her. She had a real rough time as a child. When she was a little girl she was hit by a car and needed surgery."

Suddenly a voice from the past told Roger that this was the same little girl he helped collect money for. He quickly went to his files and found the paperwork from 20 years ago and a picture of the little girl. The next day he approached Elvia and told her this story. He then showed her the picture of the little girl—it was Elvia.

Listen up!

THE MORAL OF THE STORY

1. **A good story gets better when it's personal**.
This is especially true for Roger and the employees at Armstrong International in Belgium. They can take pride in knowing that they helped to change this little girl's life for the better. This must be one of their favorite stories. Stories of fiction and make-believe don't touch the hearts and souls of our employees like a personal story does.

2. **Stories foster relationships**.
This story can only help to improve the relationship between Elvia and all the people at Armstrong International. Many have forgotten what they did so long

ago. New employees hired during this 20-year period have never heard this story. Stories must be retold or they are forgotten.

74.

VIDEO STORY

"*L*ights, Camera, Action!" The camera begins to roll and it zooms in on me sitting in a soft leather chair. To the right of me sits a lamp with the light bulb burning brightly, and neatly positioned on the coffee table sits a glass of water half-full. In my hands is my book, <u>How To Turn Your Company's Parables Into Profit</u>. I begin, "The quote to this story 'Knowing is not the same as believing'. Moral Number One." Fifteen minutes later, "That's a wrap!!" shouts the cameraman. I remember watching my first *video stories* and I thought they were pretty good, as did others.

One day, while we were shooting a new *video story* about golf carts painted as fast animals, I had the idea "Instead of sitting in a soft leather chair, why don't I tell the quote and morals to this story by using props in the story? Why don't I tell the morals while sitting on one of the animal golf carts?" So, I drove the golf cart into the view of the camera, stopped, and told the morals as the camera zoomed in on me and the animal's face. (You can see this at www.armintl.com/stories/funvideo.php3 and click on "Paw Tracks"). This action made the tape more entertaining, and at that point, I realized our video stories should not only be educational, but entertaining as well.

I had several stories on video when I came up with another idea. "While using the props in the story, I would hide the written morals in the prop so I could refresh my memory while keeping these cheat notes hidden." You see, I could use a tele-prompt by the camera, or cue cards, but unless you are a professional actor (which most business people are not) you can see my eyes move as I read the cards or tele-prompt. By hiding the morals, you don't know I'm reading them because I use the prop in a natural way, which allows me to read the next moral and then turn back to the camera and begin telling the moral. Once again, we had found a way to improve our video stories.

> Video stories bring pride to life.

THE MORAL OF THE STORY

1. **Video Stories create a feeling of identity in companies.**
Everybody likes to see their name in print. Most like to see themselves on television. It's a proud moment for that employee. A star is born. A lot of attention is given to them by co-workers and management. They have identity.

2. **Video Stories help in this age of information overload.**
It's memorable! It's fun to watch. Video stories keep your interest and entertain you, thus helping you remember the story. Today we have so much information sent to us that we become confused and paralyzed while shuffling papers, reading our faxes and e-mail. The last thing any of us want to do is <u>read</u> something, but watching a video story—hmmmmmm—Okay!

75.

PINOCCHIO

Once upon a time there was a wooden puppet whose name was Pinocchio. Pinocchio wanted to become a real live boy. One night Pinocchio's Godmother sprinkled pixie dust on him and he jumped to life.

Once upon our time, a wooden Inverted Bucket Steam Trap was hand-carved by an Armstrong customer. The wooden steam trap wanted to become a real live steam trap. We need steam, not pixie dust, to bring it to life.

Pixie dust didn't create this wooden steam trap. It took the sweat of Mike Ulmer from Caterpillar Tractor Company to turn a piece of cherry wood into a steam trap. Mike created this masterpiece from memory, which was not difficult since his company has purchased a large number of Armstrong Steam Traps.

When you wish upon a star.....

THE MORAL OF THE STORY

1. **Pursue customers who can make work "fun."**
Do business with people or companies you like. Make the experience of buying Armstrong products fun. Make Armstrong University a fun place in which to learn. Mike's

boss, Ron Luttrell, has done a great job in giving Mike opportunities to have fun at work.

2. **"For the things that are seen are temporary, but the things which are not seen are eternal." — 2 Corinthians 4:18.**
The *quality* of Armstrong Steam Traps, the *quick delivery*, the *service call* made and the *new product* introduced to customers can be seen—but are temporary. The *honesty* of our people, the *friendship* towards customers and the *fun* customers have doing business with Armstrong, are felt and remembered by our customers for a lifetime. Mike carved this steam trap because we touched his heart while he visited our factory.

3. **Stories are memorable.**
You are right! The Godmother was used in Disney's story "Cinderella" and pixie dust was used by Tinkerbell in "Peter Pan." Pinocchio came to life with a wish upon a star. You see stories are memorable. So use them in your company.

4. **Story props for my office.**
Remember my story, "David's Office" found in Once Told, They're Gold? This wooden steam trap is now in my office waiting for somebody to ask me why I have it.

Let me tell you the story about Pinocchio…

76.

SURVIVORS FOUND

The sun sat high in the sky trying to throw its warm rays to the earth through sailing snow showers. The wind was blowing hard that day. The passengers on the commercial jet were expecting a ride that would rival one at an amusement park. As the jet took the runway for takeoff, the pilot applied full takeoff power to cut through the strong winds. The power was not enough to prevent tragedy, and the plane crashed to the ground.

Sirens rang out as fire trucks raced toward the accident. Once on the scene, firemen looked for survivors among the wreckage. Several were found, but there were many fatalities. The news media was quick to tell the public of this tragic story. Family members from around the country began calling to find out if their loved ones were on the plane. Hours after the crash, it was confirmed that Dick Verheul, Vice President of Corporate Development for Armstrong International, was a passenger, and had suffered fatal injuries.

Dick Verheul is remembered through this story.

THE MORAL OF THE STORY

1. **He who refuses to remedy a wrong is guilty of a second wrong. – Mencius, Chinese Sage.**
We almost had two other executives on that same flight with Dick. Since then, we established a <u>new</u> policy which prevents certain people from flying together in case of another plane crash.

2. **Stories become sources of knowledge.**
Did you know that Armstrong-Hunt, Everlasting Valve and Warrick Controls were some of the acquisitions Dick made? His efforts live on as these companies continue to grow and prosper.

77.

SCOUT'S HONOR

This story needs to be told. It's about all the volunteers who donate their time to the Boy Scouts of America. Every story has its hero, and the hero of this story is Jack Van Scoik, who works at Armstrong International in the Assembly Department. From August 11-14, 1999 Jack volunteered to be the adult supervisor for many Boy Scouts who would attend summer camp at Rota-Kiwan. There are over 19,000 Scouts and Scouters within the Southwest Michigan Council who need heroes like Jack. Jack is just one of many heroes. So you ask, 'Why do I write this story about Jack?' Jack brought honor to Armstrong International by working with the children in the community. This story was told to me by Robert Ziegler who is the Scout Executive, so I know it to be true. Now we all know what Jack does in his spare time.

A true story.......scouts honor.

THE MORAL OF THE STORY

1. **Praise in public.......or by a story.**
I received a letter from Boy Scouts of America asking me as Jack's employer to thank him on their behalf. I've done this by writing this story.

2. **Is a story personal enough?**
It is if you hand-deliver it. I gave Jack his story in person. It was framed with a penned note in my handwriting next to the title.

STORIES
ABOUT
TRADITION

CHAPTER 16

78.

911

Dedicated to the firefighters and rescue workers of Armstrong

---

Have you ever been in a situation where your house was on fire and you needed the fire department's help? Have you ever been in an accident and needed a rescuer to come to your assistance? When we dial 911 do we ever ask where these volunteers come from? Many of them come from Armstrong International. These people are full-time employees, but Armstrong still supports and encourages these volunteers to leave work at any time to rescue an accident victim or to put out a fire.

Just the other day I witnessed several Armstrong volunteers running to their cars. Their radios were blasting with the location of an accident. I heard car engines running, emergency lights were flashing red and white. Cars were pulling out of the parking lot in a quick race for the accident scene. As I watched this, I realized that a story needed to be told about these special volunteers. We also need to let Armstrongers know what the company policy is on volunteering during company time for aiding at fire and accident scenes. For over 20 years, Armstrong's legend of supporting and paying Armstrong's volunteers who put out fires and help accident victims, has flourished. Like all great legends, it will continue to live.

An Armstrong tradition to be proud of.

THE MORAL OF THE STORY

1. **A tradition to be proud of.**
The Fire Association (composed of Lockport-Fabius-Park Townships Firefighters) recently voted, unanimously, to recognize Armstrong International for its long-standing support, by presenting the company with a plaque of appreciation for 20 plus years of support. Randy Huyck, Armstrong employee, who also acts as Fire Chief of Lockport-Fabius Park Townships Fire Department, presented the award. "The guys all wanted to do something special to recognize Armstrong for its continued support of our efforts," Huyck revealed. "It is our way of thanking Armstrong International for supporting yet another very important element of the community."

2. **"A business that makes nothing but money is a poor kind of business,"– Henry Ford.**
Yes, it costs money to allow our work force to volunteer during work hours. We lose productivity, but we feel the price we pay will help improve our community. God put us on this earth to help others in need.

3. **False Alarms.**
Armstrong International will not pay you your full salary if you leave work as a volunteer. Armstrong will pay the difference between your volunteer pay and what you make while at work. You will not lose any pay but you will benefit as a volunteer knowing you did your community service.

79.
LIKE FATHER LIKE SON

Long ago, Leo Wright was responsible for maintaining the grounds of Armstrong Machine Works. I remember seeing Leo ride the yellow lawn mower as he cut the grass. In the autumn, I would watch him raking up leaves. During the winter, Leo would throw salt down on all the sidewalks so Armstrong employees would not fall on sheets of ice. Leo retired from Armstrong many years ago and Fred Newbre took his place.

Armstrong International had grown, increasing the amount of grass to be mowed, yards to be raked, and sidewalks to be salted, but Fred kept up. Just recently Richard Wright took over the duties for Fred who moved back into the factory. I saw Richard mowing the grass the other day. It brought back pleasant memories; memories from the past when I saw his father mowing that same yard of grass. I thought, "Can I write a story about mowing grass? No, but I can write a story about a father and son who have both worked at Armstrong."

The apple doesn't fall far from the tree.

THE MORAL OF THE STORY

1. **Like father like son.**
We want our employee's children to come to work for Armstrong International. If the parent is a talented, hard-working employee, there's a good chance that the child will be just like their parent. When recruiting employees, it is always challenging to determine if they will fit in Armstrong's culture. When you hire a son or daughter of an employee, you know they understand the culture of Armstrong. They grew up with it. Before accepting a job, the child will also know if the company believes in the same ethics, community involvement, job security, etc., a win-win situation for both employer and employee.

2. **Imagine working for a company when you can't wait for your son or daughter to work there.**
You want to know if our employee's have pride in where they work? See if they encourage their children to work for Armstrong. I can think of no better test of the morale of our people than to check the company phone directory for common last names.

3. **Be careful what you say and to whom . . .** it may be a family member.
I am referring to gossip and negative comments made about co-workers. You have to work side by side, and for what I hope will be a very long time. The last thing you need is to make some smart remark because of angry emotions, or a disagreement. Remember, a father's pride and protection for his child does not stop at home, but is for all time in all places — even work. I am not saying that we cannot

discipline a son or daughter, but that we should be careful how we say it.

4. 'Til Death Do Us Part.

Don't forget about those Armstrong employees who are husband and wife. We have quite a few. Again, I don't think anybody would encourage their spouse to work at Armstrong if they weren't proud of where they worked.

5. Second generation employees.

Fred Newbre and his son, Lester Newbre, along with Leo Wright and his son, Richard Wright, can be proud that they have two generations of their family working at Armstrong International.

The record, however, is held by the Kauffmans and Hartmans. The Kauffmans legacy began with Maxine Dyer, her daughter, Marsha, son-in-law Charlie Kauffman, and grandson, Jeff Kauffman. The Hartmans record started with Forrest Hartman, William Hartman, and David Hartman. OOPS . . . make the record four generations: Adam Armstrong, Lawrence Armstrong, Gus Armstrong, David and Patrick Armstrong.

80.

CHOCOLATE CHIP COOKIES

They ate happily ever after. You knew who they were because you could see the cookie crumbs and chocolate on their lips. If you've never tasted Etta Griffin's chocolate chip cookies, you don't know what you've been missing. Once a year, Etta bakes cookies for the <u>first</u> department that reaches it's giving goal of 100%. Etta's cookies have become such a prize that Armstrong's punch press department reached its 1997 departmental 100% giving goal just 30 minutes after they had received their pledge cards.

    Let's go back to the beginning of this story when the cookies were still in the oven. It has always been a long-time tradition for Armstrong employees to support the area in which they live and work. Each year Armstrong International and its employees provide a generous donation to the Community Chest. Even some Armstrong retirees have come forward and given contributions. What makes this story so special is not just the donation to the Community Chest, but the fact that Armstrong International and its employees try to get 100% participation. With 288 full-time employees, this is no easy task. Etta's famous chocolate chip cookies help to get the pledge cards returned quickly.

A secret recipe.

THE MORAL OF THE STORY

1. **The selfish person cannot understand the unselfish person.**
The selfish employee cannot understand the unselfish Company. Armstrong International has very few selfish employees. That's important because there is harmony between Armstrong International and its employees. The relationship is peaceful. Remember the moral to one of Aesop's Fables, "Birds of a Feather flock together."

2. **Well done is better than well said. — Ben Franklin.**
For decades, Armstrongers have pledged 100% (or very close) in donations to the Community Chest. Etta Griffin has served on the Community Chest drive for 17 years, and has been on the board of directors for the last six years. Well done, Etta.

3. **A way of life!**
When it comes to supporting local charitable causes, local schools, various fund raising events, and the community of Three Rivers, Michigan, Armstrong International and it's employees have always tried to give. It's a way of life! This way of life continues because we hire unselfish people. If Armstrong and its employees support local charities, just imagine what they will do for those who pay them — you know, the <u>customers.</u>

81.

ARMSTRONG TRAP MAGAZINE

This story recalls the time when Armstrong Trap Magazine was first introduced. It was late November 1931. Armstrong Trap Magazine was published by Armstrong Machine Works four times a year. The magazine had case histories, technical articles and new product/service articles. Our sales force (representatives) provided mailing lists, leads for case histories, helped pay the cost, and replied to customer needs. A total of 70,000 copies were sent out every three months.

    Now we will remember when the Armstrong Trap Magazine was replaced. The year was 1999 and web sites on the Internet were popular. More and more of our customers, especially the young ones who had grown up in the computer age, were turning to the web page of Armstrong International and not to Armstrong Trap Magazine. The cost of Armstrong Trap Magazine was quite high, and keeping up the names and addresses of over 70,000 customers was time consuming. The Armstrong Trap Magazine was a tradition at Armstrong Machine Works. It had been around for 68 years—a very old tradition. It was very difficult to stop printing the magazine, but that is what we did in 1999.

Knowledge not shared is energy wasted™.

THE MORAL OF THE STORY

1. **If you have knowledge, let others light their candles by it.**
Armstrong International has always believed in sharing its steam knowledge with customers. Armstrong Trap Magazine was just one of many ways we shared this knowledge. The tradition was not the Armstrong Trap Magazine, but the steam knowledge we shared. This tradition will continue. We will use Armstrong Service, Armstrong University, product literature and our web site to share this knowledge and keep the tradition alive.

2. **www.armstrong-intl.com**
Armstrong customers could not find Armstrong Trap Magazine on the Internet. A survey revealed that the times had changed the way our customers wanted technical information shared. The Internet replaced our popular magazine. We changed the way our tradition was shared so it would live another 68 years.

3. **It takes time to build tradition.**
Traditions normally become stronger with the passage of time. Armstrong Trap Magazine was a very strong tradition after 68 years of publication. There were a lot of people opposed to canceling the magazine. They thought this would be unwise. Our customers would rebel. I was not afraid to kill the Armstrong Trap Magazine in 1999 because Armstrong Trap Magazine was not the tradition, but the information on its pages was. Once people understood this, it was easier to cancel Armstrong Trap Magazine. If you

refer to my story "Our Company Picnic" in my book <u>How To Turn Your Parables Into Profit</u>, moral 4, you will remember that I talked about being careful not to change your traditions to save money. We changed this tradition to bring it to life, not to save a few dollars. Remember to properly identify what your tradition is before you say you cannot change it. This tradition was not about the Armstrong Trap Magazine but about sharing knowledge.

82.

ALLIGATOR BRIEFCASE

"Please find your seat and stow your bags carefully in the bins above you, or under the seat in front of you," announced the flight attendant.

While sitting in my seat, I watched the people board the airplane and march down the aisle with bags in hand. A young man stopped beside me and placed an alligator briefcase in the bin above me. Another person behind him also had an alligator briefcase and carefully stowed it away. The man sat down next to me.

"I like your briefcase, is that really alligator?"

"No, it's imitation, but a long time ago Upjohn did give real alligator bags to its salespeople."

"You mean Upjohn gives alligator bags to all their employees that travel?"

"Yes, everybody."

"I always wondered why I saw so many alligator bags on the airplanes, especially in Kalamazoo, Michigan."

"You'll see more in Kalamazoo because that is where our company is located." Just then a lady bumps my shoulder with her bag, and, of course, it was another alligator bag.

You create a tradition in a few seconds, and maintain it for a lifetime.

STORIES ABOUT TRADITION

THE MORAL OF THE STORY

1. **The sweet smell of success.**
When we see alligator shoes or an alligator belt, the perception of that person is they are successful because alligator is expensive. The same is true when you see an alligator briefcase. That <u>company</u> must be successful. Customers like doing business with a salesperson that represents a successful company. It shows that the company will be able to service their customer. The employees take comfort in knowing their company is making money, which in turn will keep them employed. The alligator briefcase is a tradition at Upjohn. If management does away with this tradition the customers and employees may think the company is no longer successful. It may not be true, but if the alligator briefcases become extinct, customers and employees may become extinct.

2. **Armstrong wooden briefcases.**
Jim Daugherty, TESTS-Я-US Manager, also does wonderful things with wood. I had Jim make me a wooden briefcase out of Chamfered wood and the Armstrong logo inlayed in a different wood. Every time I fly, people ask me about my briefcase. I have thought about making the wooden briefcase the official briefcase for Armstrong International. They are expensive and hold less paper than expandable briefcases. I know the power of a tradition — I also know how much it can cost. We must always be careful about starting a new tradition because with the passage of time it becomes the brick and mortar of your company. Very hard to change.

STORIES ABOUT LEGENDS AND TALL TALES

CHAPTER 17

83.
ALOHA

This story begins with the ending of my mother's life. Her four-year battle with cancer had come to an end. As with all funerals, a customary viewing was held in Stuart, Florida. While standing in the funeral home and accepting condolences from friends and family, I couldn't help but notice all the flowers in the parlor. The flowers were tropical and it reminded me of Hawaii. My thoughts took me back to the sales convention Armstrong held in Hawaii and the fun we had with my mother there. Suddenly, I heard a familiar voice.

"Aloha, David."

I turned around and for a minute I was startled, then I recognized the familiar face. It was Rusty LeBeau.

"Aloha, Rusty."

"I am so sorry about your loss. Your mother was a great woman. I had to come and pay my respects."

"Thank you, Rusty. I know you were special to her." Then it dawned on me, "Don't you live in Hawaii?"

"Yes, but I had to come, your mother was special to me, too."

"Wow. You get the longest trip award." Just then my father came up and tapped Rusty on the shoulder.

"Hello Rusty."

"Gus, I am so sorry for your loss."

"She would be happy that you came. We're all going to miss her. Rusty, are you still in the hotel business?"

"Yes, I'm working for Westin again."

"I bet they're keeping you busy."

"They sure are. I just returned to Hawaii from Florida when I got the news about your wife, Gus. I took a quick shower and hopped back on the plane and flew right back over."

I interrupted, "You did WHAT? Did I hear you correctly? You just returned to Hawaii from a long trip in Florida, and hopped right back on a plane and flew back to Florida?"

"That's ok. I wanted to say goodbye to your mother."

It's lonely at the top, only if you want it to be.

THE MORAL OF THE STORY

1. **"Celebrations are wonderful arenas for bonding." — Tom Peters.**
Mom was truly a legend when it came to meeting people and remembering their names. In 1991, Armstrong held a convention in Hawaii. Mom organized it, as always, and worked very closely with Rusty, who worked at the Westin Hotel. A great friendship grew between mom and Rusty. Many years later mom hired Rusty to run the hotel business for Armstrong Service.

2. **Legends are created and known by the stories told.**
If you turn to the back of this book under the chapter Rookie Storytellers, and look for the story, "A Trip To Remember" you will read of a story which confirms why my mother was a legend. Another story titled, "Dirty Fingernails" found in my book How To Turn Your Parables

Into Profit is yet another story confirming her as a legend in her time.

3. **The secret of being a legend is not doing what one must, but doing what one loves to do.**
Mom loved to meet people, entertain them, get to know them, and be their friend. This was not a job, this was part of her being. Sometimes mom's friendship made things difficult for her. I remember the time she had to tell Rusty (after he had been working for Armstrong Service for two years) that he was no longer needed because Armstrong's hotel business was not yet ready. She was able to do this without damaging their friendship, and that's the rest of this story.

84.

BILL DRUMM'S HOUSE MORTGAGE

Two strawberry and one vanilla milkshakes sat on the table. Surrounding the table were three men telling stories. Frank Blossom and Harry Wilson from Intelitouch were responsible for creating and telling stories in their company. They had hired six professional writers. They had heard about my storytelling over the last decade and had come to visit Armstrong International. As we sat at the table, they were asking me questions.

"If you don't have professional storytellers, who writes the stories?"

"I write the stories. Sometimes I have rookie storytellers in my company who write stories. The stories are about Armstrong International. That's all I really write about."

"Where do you find the stories?"

"That's a good question. It depends on what kind of story I want to write. In my second book, <u>How To Turn Your Company's Parables Into Profit</u>, I explain where to find stories and how to write them."

We each lifted the milkshakes and took another drink. Then I felt a tap on my shoulder. I turned around.

"Hi David, how have you been?"

"Hi Bill. How's retirement treating you?"

"Just fine."

"You used to work in the repair parts department didn't you?"

"That's right."

I introduced Bill Drumm to each of the people at the table.

"Armstrong's a great company," said Bill. "I worked there for 44 years."

"44 years?!"

"Yes sir, 44 years. I remember when Adam Armstrong would walk through the shop and office once a month. He'd ask everybody if they had any financial needs. Or, if there was anything he could do for them."

"Bill, did he ever come by your bench and ask if you needed help?"

"Of course, David."

"Did you ever need any help?"

"I remember once I was right out of school, not very old, and I needed a down-payment for my house. I had just gotten married. Adam gave me $3,800. That was in 1944. A few years later, my wife sold her house and we were able to pay Adam back. I remember walking in and sitting down in front of his big desk. I placed a large stack of money in front of him. Then I placed a second stack of money on the desk.

Adam looked at the stacks and pointed to the first one and said, "What's that?"

"That's the loan I owe you."

Then Adam pointed to the second stack and said, "Then what's that?"

"That's the interest I owe you." Adam gently pushed the interest money back towards me and said, "I don't want that".

When Bill left, I turned to Frank and Harry, smiling and said, "Just another story to add to my books. A great story."

> *A righteous man loans money without interest.*
> *1000 Proverbs*

THE MORAL OF THE STORY

1. **Stories reveal values of a leader.**
Would you want to work for Adam Armstrong? What do you think of Adam Armstrong after hearing this story? The founders of companies normally become legends. Thomas Edison, Henry Ford, Walt Disney and Bill Gates are just a few that come to mind. You too can be a legend in your company. You do not have to be the founder. You must do something that is truly special and memorable—and it doesn't have to cost a lot of money. Work on becoming a legend in your company like Barbara Armstrong did in the previous story, "Aloha". Remember, Barbara was not the founder but still a true legend

85.

LAYOFF

Beginning next week there will be a layoff. Due to the slowdown in the economy, which resulted in lost sales, we are forced to reduce the work force by 25%. The company regrets taking this action and will do everything within its power to hire those Armstrongers laid-off when orders increase.

Jeff Boynton became sick to his stomach when he read this. It would be the third layoff that he would go through in a 13-year period. He had been fortunate in the past two layoffs to find a part-time job until the company hired him back, but this layoff was different. He now had a family and a baby on the way. What would he do? He was no longer single. It was time to go out and look for a full-time job, not a part-time job until he was hired back. He submitted his resume to several places, one of which was Armstrong International, where his father, Terry Boynton, had previously worked. Before long the layoff had come to an end and he was re-hired.

Two years later, Armstrong International contacted Jeff and wanted to know if he was still interested in employment. Ken Clay, Personnel Director, informed Jeff that there was an opening in the HVAC department of Armstrong International. Jeff couldn't believe his ears. "Why yes, I'm interested in working at Armstrong."

> *I posted this story on Armstrong bulletin boards. It looked authentic.*

THE MORAL OF THE STORY

1. **Did your heart skip a beat when you read the title to this story, "Layoff"?**
Did the first two sentences concern you? Did you think you were going to be laid off at Armstrong International? I apologize if I scared you. I would never do that intentionally, but that was the title of my story. All right, I confess that the only way I could get you to feel the shock and panic that Jeff experienced was to lure you into believing it was happening to you, even if it was only for a few brief moments.

2. **The best way to appreciate your job is to imagine yourself without it.**
Don't take job security for granted. I know Andy Shirk doesn't. Many months ago Andy told me that he had been offered a job at higher pay but turned it down. I asked Andy, "why"? "The job security at Armstrong is worth something. The peace of mind I have knowing that my family will be provided for is worth more than a few extra dollars in my paycheck. Actually, it was several dollars more." Andy, like Jeff, appreciates job security. Do you? Not too long ago I heard rumors that a few Armstrongers were considering leaving for better pay. A local company was paying a signing bonus, big bucks, and plenty of overtime. This same company has a history of layoffs. We have only lost three employees to them over the years. Remember this story; remember how you felt when you read the title; remember how you felt while reading the first

two lines, and remember that job security should not be taken for granted.

86.

A FEATHER IN OUR HAT

It is indeed an honor for Armstrong International to be recognized as Business of The Year by the Better Business Bureau of Western Michigan. That was the case in 1998 and we are pleased to announce at the awards ceremonies held in the year 2000 the Better Business Bureau Business of The Year is once again Armstrong International. On a national scale, Armstrong International was the only Michigan based company to make the prestigious list of 22 finalists for the 1999 Council of Better Business Bureau's National Torch Award for marketplace ethics. Our goal as a company is not to win awards, but when we receive them it confirms our dedication to excellence in how we do business and how we value our employees and all those we serve.

A Peacock today may be a feather duster tomorrow.

THE MORAL OF THE STORY

1. **Pride blinds us.**
We should be proud of what we have accomplished but not be complacent. This can happen because once a company has won an award it is deceived into believing it is the best

now and <u>forever</u>. Maybe that was true on a given day, but not forever.

2. **Consistency is a plus.**
Armstrong has not received just one award, but many – I haven't even mentioned that we were named "Best in Community Service" by the Better Business Bureau in 1996 and received a prestigious award from the Three Rivers Chamber of Commerce in 1998 for "Best in Community Service and Involvement." It's interesting that in every year the company was nominated for an award, it took top honors. Not a bad track record. However, Armstrong International is only as good as its people. All the awards we have been recognized for are a direct result and true reflection of the great team we have at Armstrong International. We are all proud to be Armstrongers and it shows in our actions.

3. **So has pride blinded us?**
I believe the answer is no. We have not rested on our laurels for 101 years, and don't intend to now. Heck, with that kind of a track record, what should I be worried about? What a great group of people we have at Armstrong International – a blessing for sure. And it's nice to see that unbiased parties outside our company see that too, as evidenced by the many awards we've received.

ARMSTRONG FABLES

INTRODUCTION

In my quest to continue telling stories in the business world, I have created a new chapter titled Armstrong Fables. These fables are things we don't do well at Armstrong. Events we may not be proud of.

Fables are stories about animals that take on human characteristics. Every owl is wise, every turtle is slow, and every fox is clever. Immediately the reader will know something about the personality of the character in the story, but will not be able to identify who the person is. Continue to read my stories and follow the morals so you do not become an Armstrong Fable.

87.
THE GOAT AMONGST THE SHEEP

Outside a small town there lived a herd of sheep. These sheep were good-natured; willing to help each other and respectful of each other's possessions. A very old shepherd watched over the sheep. The shepherd was proud of his sheep. He built a special place where the sheep, at the end of a hard day's journey, could relax, celebrate and play. The shepherd had provided many toys for his sheep. The sheep were grateful, and enjoyed their special place by taking care of it with pride.

Throughout the years the herd grew, but something changed. There were now goats mixed in the herd. A few kids, children of the goats, had also joined the herd. These kids did not respect the special place the shepherd had built. They damaged and misused the toys. They left things in a mess, and their attitude was very unbecoming. Now, these kids thought nobody knew who they were, but they were sadly mistaken. The shepherd knew who the kids were, and it was only a matter of time before he would remove them from his herd of sheep.

Align your company with employees who share its values.

THE MORAL OF THE STORY

1. **You can run, but you can't hide.**
We will not let a few bad employees children (kids) who damage the toys in the Armstrong Recreation Building, prevent us from buying more toys in fear that they too might be damaged. We will identify those kids who are damaging the toys and remove them.

2. **Do you remember all of the stories I told you about self-management and trust?**
Armstrong International (the shepherd) insists on its employees being trustworthy and self-managing. Re-read my stories: "From Rages to Riches", "The President's Son Is Late For Work", "Did You Close the Window?", and "Playing Hooky".

3. **Goat's milk anybody?**
Have you ever tasted goat milk? YUCK!! Few like it. Be careful that you are not one of these goats who nobody likes. Make sure that no one in your family is misusing the equipment in the recreation building, because it's only a matter of time before you or your kids are identified as the goats of Armstrong International.

4. **Baaaha, baaaha.**
Sometimes the shepherd needs the sheep to speak up. You good sheep have witnessed goats misusing or destroying YOUR toys. Stop them! At the very least, tell the shepherd who they are. Remember, self-management is always best, but sometimes needs a little help.

88.

THE FOXES AND THE HUNTER

Have you heard the Armstrong fable about the foxes and the hunter? It begins with the bravest fox talking to the hunter.

"If you want us to be more clever and fun to hunt, you need to give us windows so we may see outside and plan our escape."

"No," replied the hunter. "It would be much too expensive to add windows to your den."

"Well then, how about new carpet so our claws can grow sharp instead of being worn down from the hard floor. This would make us faster during the hunt."

"No," replied the hunter. "You are much too fast already."

"Could you paint the doors to our den so that you and the other hunters might find us for the hunt?"

"Consider it done," replied the hunter.

More than six months had passed and nothing had been done to the door. The foxes became angry. They decided to take things into their own hands. They quickly found paintbrushes and began to paint graffiti, without profanity, on the doors. They waited to see what would happen. The hunter immediately saw the graffiti and became concerned. "Stupid foxes! I'll just have somebody paint over the graffiti." The hunter quickly assigned somebody to paint the doors.

As clever as a fox.

THE MORAL OF THE STORY

1. **Armstrong Graffiti**.
Several Armstrongers (the foxes) were unhappy with the appearance of their department. They had complained to Armstrong management (the hunter), but nothing had been done, even after they were told, **Consider it Done!** After complaining repeatedly, they decided to get clever and outsmart management. "Surely if we paint the doors with graffiti, management will have to repaint them."

2. **"Well begun is half done."**
Aristotle's wisdom still applies today. Management (the hunter) began well by listening to the employees (foxes), however, management did not finish what it started.

3. **Would you be upset if your employees painted graffiti?**
Several Armstrong leaders were upset. I laughed and found it rewarding that some Armstrongers were creative enough to get their leaders' attention after they failed to do what they promised. I'm not saying that the leaders were at fault. They have many priorities, but I do think after six months the doors could have been painted. The foxes could have painted the doors instead of painting graffiti on them. This Armstrong fable is <u>not</u> about placing blame on the hunter or the foxes. It's about creativity and urgency.

4. **A great remedy for anger is fun**.
I'm sure these Armstrongers had fun painting graffiti on their doors. I hope this made them feel better and not

completely helpless. They meant no harm. Maybe they have read too many stories by David Armstrong, hoping that he would enjoy their creative solution. I like the way they dealt with their anger. It's more productive than other examples I've seen. Oh, I was the hunter who said **Consider It Done**. I assigned it but failed to follow up -- it was my <u>word</u>.

89.

THE TURTLE AND THE FISHERMAN

Once upon a time there was a turtle who was sunning herself on a rock. The rock was high upon a hill, and the water splashed below. The turtle watched carefully as off in the distance a fisherman pushed off from shore in a rowboat. The fisherman slowly rowed his way towards the rock where the turtle sunned.

"Ah, the sun feels so good," smiled the turtle. "I have plenty of time. He will never get here in time to catch me. I'm much too fast."

A few minutes passed. The turtle lifted her neck into the air, stretching it long, and looked over to see how close the fisherman was.

"Still not close enough for me to run to the water. He will never catch me."

She closes her eyes. A few minutes later she is startled when she hears a noise. Putt-putt-putt. The turtle quickly looks up to where the fisherman with the oars was, but there's no noise. He's still slowly rowing towards the turtle. The turtle then looks to her right, and sees a fisherman coming at her, full speed with an outboard motor. The turtle quickly races to the edge of the rock, and just as she leaps for the water, the fisherman's net catches her.

Turtle soup, anyone?

THE MORAL OF THE STORY

1. **There is no job so simple that it cannot be done wrong.**
I saw a memo one day from one Armstronger to another. It said, *"I talked to the vendor and they say there is nothing they can do to improve the 14 week delivery time. This is after they receive the <u>approved</u> drawings. The sooner Armstrong places the order, the quicker we will get it."* The Armstronger finished by adding a special comment to the other Armstronger: *"Please remember there is some internal process time here at Armstrong, which usually takes a week."* I went bonkers when I read this. These Armstrongers (turtles) need a good kick in the tail. How can it take these Armstrongers a week to approve a drawing before placing the order to the vendor? I made some calls. This is what I found: It only took approximately 45 minutes to do all the functions within Armstrong before placing the order with the vendor. The real problem was the inter-company mail (the brown envelope) took 4 days, 7 hours and 15 minutes to be delivered between departments. Delivering intercompany mail is simple, yet we screwed it up!

2. **Those who ignore the past are doomed to repeat it.**
Either do away with the internal mail system, or make it better and faster. No more turtle soup. I'm full!

3. **Wooden oars versus outboard motors.**
Intercompany mail versus networking within Armstrong's computer system. We have the technology within our

company to share information quickly through our network. We do not need to continue to use inter-company mail. It's too slow. There will be a competitor out there, like the fisherman with the outboard motor, who will beat us to our lunch if we don't use the technology we've **invested** in.

90.

THE GEESE AND THEIR COFFEE

There was once a flock of geese who were very trusting neighbors. The geese took great pride in making coffee for their neighbors, who in turn, would pay the geese on the honor system for each cup they took. The geese always left the coffee brewing on the counter. Sometimes they flew out on errands, leaving a can of coffee available for brewing.

One day, while flying in formation towards their home, they spotted Mr. Weasel below carrying a can of coffee under his arm. Mr. Weasel saw the flock of geese and smiled, then made a turn down another path which led to his home.

Shortly thereafter, the geese landed near a tree. Now, Mr. Owl was perched in that tree and when he heard the geese, he interrupted them, "What are you talking about?"

"We believe Mr. Weasel stole a can of coffee from our kitchen and we know he didn't pay us."

"Are you sure you weren't paid?" Asked the wise owl.

"No, but we saw him walking on the path from our home with a can of coffee. Why does he need a whole can? Besides that, we all know about Mr. Weasel's reputation. Can he really be trusted?"

"Let me go talk to Mr. Weasel and hear his side of the story." Mr. Owl flew off.

"Pardon me, Mr. Weasel, the geese are very upset with you. They think you stole some coffee."

"What kind of person do they think I am? Just because my last name is Weasel, they think the worst. I paid for the coffee!"

"Did you take the can to lower the price per cup by making your own coffee?"

"No, of course not! Several in my family like their coffee really strong and the geese don't make it strong enough. We decided to make our own. That was the only reason I bought the can of coffee."

"I will be happy to tell the geese your side of the story."

When Mr. Owl returned, he found that the geese had locked up all the coffee!! The wise owl knew that this could not go unchallenged. He instructed them to remove the locks, which they happily did once they heard the whole story.

The number one rule for trust – there are no locks!!

THE MORAL OF THE STORY

1. **Trust comes from being trusted.**
We shape the attitudes of Armstrongers by not using locks. If we use locks they become a <u>daily</u> reminder that we don't trust you. Talk about your brainwashing! Daily brainwashing!! Locks will not create trust, but they are the first step towards destroying our tradition of trust. What next––time clocks?

2. **Trusting Armstrongers is a noble thing, but it does involve risk.**
Every day we fight the urge to install locks. What we try to do few companies will ever even attempt. It would be much easier and less risky if we did not attempt to trust each other. Take comfort in knowing that Armstrong's tradition of trust will be difficult to practice but will make us stronger. Stronger because people who trust one another work best together.

3. **"A house divided against itself can not stand" – Abraham Lincoln.**
We all live under the same roof, yet there are some Armstrongers (geese) who wish to use locks because they do not trust their fellow Armstronger. If this is allowed to continue, our house will fall. <u>Every</u> Armstronger must stand for trust. When you find someone who is not trustworthy, or <u>think</u> is not trustworthy, like Mr. Weasel, you must confront them and try to persuade them to be trustworthy. If you fail, bring another Armstronger with you and together try and convince the person who is not trustworthy to change their ways. If this does not work, then approach management (Mr. Owl) and we will ask the employee to change or leave Armstrong International, because no house can stand if it is divided.

4. **Knowing when "not" to make a decision is just as important as knowing when to make a decision.**
One person who steals does not justify changing a tradition of trust and honor. Knowing this Armstrong tradition should compel <u>one not to make a decision</u> to lock up the coffee.

91.

THE PARROT WHISPERS SADNESS TO THE SHEEP

Once upon a time there was a valley where the grass grew thick and green. To this valley the shepherds would bring their flock of sheep to graze. There was one shepherd whose family had been shepherds for four generations. He knew the best places in the valley for his sheep to graze. He even found a nice bubbling brook with cool running water. A large tree provided shade near the brook. He always took his sheep there. The sheep were happy, for they believed they had the best shepherd in the valley.

One day a parrot flew from one side of the valley to the other and landed in that tree where this shepherd's sheep grazed.

"Excuse me," said the parrot "I just flew from the other side of the valley, and you should see the grass over there. It's much thicker, greener, and tastier!"

"Really," replied one of the sheep "I always thought this was the best place for grazing."

"You should see all the trees on the other side of the valley," squawked the Parrot.

"We only have one tree." frowned a sheep.

"How much do you get to eat?" asked the parrot.

"The shepherd always let me drink as much water as I want, but I don't get a chance to graze as much as I'd like."

"The other side of the valley is better — I know, I was there," announced the Parrot.

"How do you know it's better?" asked a wise sheep. "You don't eat grass!"

"That's correct," whispered the parrot, "but I was talking to the sheep of another shepherd and they told me how wonderful the grass tasted and that they can eat as much as they want. These sheep also told me what made their shepherd the best of all shepherds."

"What is it?" asked several of the sheep.

"Mind you I have only heard this, but I understand that the shepherd only shears his sheep once every two years."

"What?! We get sheared once a year!"

"I also understand that he has never had a wolf attack or lost any sheep."

Now with this the sheep became sad, and began to challenge their shepherd. The sheep were no longer happy with their parcel of land nor with the tree that gave them shade from the hot sun, nor from the cool brook that brought them cool fresh water. Once the sheep were happy with their shepherd and now they were sad. The parrot flew off to another part of the valley to whisper his sadness.

The grass is not always greener on the other side of the fence.

THE MORAL OF THE STORY

1. **If it sounds too good to be true, it probably is**.
The parrot in this fable could be an outsider or Armstronger who was talking to Armstrong employees (sheep). Now let's suppose that this person had just come from another company and was talking about how good the salary was at that company. As your leader (shepherd) Armstrong cares about each and every one of you and does the best it can to treat you fairly. Once an Armstronger is told that they could make more money at another company (eat more grass), that Armstronger will never be as happy with their job again. That's sad because at one time the sheep were very happy until that parrot flew in and whispered his gossip. I have seen a few Armstrongers take employment at other companies for a better wage and benefits, only to hear thereafter that they were fired or laid off. Be careful! Read the quote again.

2. **Who's afraid of the big bad wolf .** ♫
You should be. In this Armstrong fable you heard the parrot refer to a wolf. Lets assume this wolf is the economy which goes bad and hurts the profits of Armstrong International. At Armstrong International, we have not had a layoff, but we have killed several wolves. This has been so for almost one hundred years. Of course, we can make no promise that there won't be a layoff in the next 100 years, but it is our culture and tradition not to layoff.

3. **Do not become a bad sheep.**
Do not tell others how much your salary is. Do not tell others how big your raise was. This is one of the few policies at Armstrong International. Armstrong

International is not ashamed of how much it pays its employees. We are concerned that some employees will become disappointed when they learn that other fellow employees are making higher wages. The fact is there will always be somebody making more money than you. I have witnessed Armstrongers who were very happy with their job and salary only to become disappointed when they thought the company was paying others more or because they received a smaller raise.

92.

THE JACKAL AND THE LOYAL DOG

Once upon a time a jackal was walking through the woods when he came across a dog.

"Hi distant cousin!" said the jackal.

"Hello," barked the dog. "We should become friends. We could hunt together, protect each other from our enemies, and play together."

"I would like that very much." Replied the jackal.

A friendship was started, and day after day the jackal and dog hunted together and played together.

One day while the dog and jackal were out hunting, the jackal came across a rabbit and killed it. The dog was not in sight so the jackal thought to himself 'this is a small rabbit. Just enough food for me.' So he hid the rabbit in the woods, never telling the dog. Later that day the dog brought back a small pig, and the two feasted together. Later that night the jackal went into the woods and ate his rabbit without sharing it.

The next day came and the dog said, "Where should we hunt?"

"Lets split up." Replied the Jackal. "We will have a better chance of finding more food."

Again the jackal repeated what he had done the previous day. When the dog returned that evening with nothing, he asked the jackal how he had done. "I caught nothing." Replied the jackal. They went hungry that night until the jackal went into the woods and ate his tasty meal—alone.

One late evening as the jackal was eating his meal in private, he heard growling and barking. He decided to check it out. As he approached the noise, he saw dog fighting two other wolves. It was a fierce battle so jackal decided not to help. Jackal quietly snuck back into the woods, hoping not to be seen by his friend. Dog won the battle and as he licked his wounds, he knew that jackal was no longer his friend. He had seen jackal hiding in the woods never offering to help.

Dishonesty will be terminated. Thieves prosecuted.

THE MORAL OF THE STORY

1. **No customer's credit is as good as its money.**
Armstrong has befriended a Jackal. Mr. Jackal was a partner for <u>many decades</u>. Over time, Mr. Jackal got into financial trouble. Armstrong gave financial help for over five years. Mr. Jackal continued to fall behind in his payments to Armstrong so we put him on C.O.D. (cash on delivery). Customers stopped buying our products because Mr. Jackal told them Armstrong had delivery problems instead of the truth, which was he couldn't get products because he didn't have cash to pay C.O.D. Mr. Jackal hurt our market share and company image. Over time, we learned that Mr. Jackal would never pay Armstrong for services and products delivered. Our partner (Jackal) took advantage of our friendship and our loyalty. Thieves will be prosecuted.

2. **A jackal keeping food (profits) to himself will be the end of a friendship**.
We found out that Mr. Jackal was charging very high prices to our customers while asking for <u>extra</u> discounts from Armstrong due to competitive prices. We ended the contract with him because he lied.

3. **A jackal hiding in the woods will be seen—sooner or later**.
Mr. Jackal became the enemy when he started selling copies of Armstrong products and lead customers to believe the products were made by Armstrong. He didn't think we would see him—we did. Thieves will be prosecuted.

93.

THE BLACK COLT AND THE BROWN COLT

This fable begins with a black mare giving birth to a black colt. In the stall next to her, a few minutes later, a brown mare had just given birth to a brown colt. The owner of the mares was very proud of his new racehorses. The owner decided to train the black colt, and hired another trainer to work with the brown colt. The brown colt was moved to Kentucky, where the trainer lived. For the next two years both colts worked hard at becoming faster so that one day they could race in the Kentucky Derby. During these two years, the black colt had won many races across the country. The brown colt had won only a few races. It was the day before the Kentucky Derby and there was a last minute cancellation. The owner received a call to see if he had a horse to race. "Why yes!" He shouted in joy. The owner only had 24 hours to have the horse at the race. He chose the brown horse.

Everybody wants to be promoted. Not always true.

THE MORAL OF THE STORY

1. **Armstrongers get promoted because they have earned it.**
Not always true! Being in the right place at the right time may also be just as important. The brown colt was promoted to the Kentucky Derby because he was already in Kentucky and the owner didn't have time to transport the black colt.

2. **Armstrongers who have success story after success story, in regards to their performance, are the ones who get promoted.**
Not always true! The black colt had won more races than the brown colt. Sometimes the owner (Armstrong International) is looking for creativity, or for someone who promotes urgency and not someone who has many successes.

3. **Armstrongers who know the right person get promoted.**
Not always true! Sometimes being the friend of the boss, or a family member of the boss, delays a promotion. The black colt received his training from the owner. Was the black colt selected? No, the brown colt was. Sometimes the owner will be extra cautious in giving a promotion to family or friends so the people do not feel that there is favoritism being shown.

4. **Armstrongers who have long years of service are promoted.**
Not always true! Remember, the black colt was born first, but the brown colt got promoted to the Kentucky Derby. It

doesn't matter if you have 20 years of service with the company, or two years. If somebody has the skills we need, they may be promoted before someone who only has more years of service.

5. **Armstrongers who are willing to move get promoted.** Not always true! In this fable, the black colt wasn't even given a chance to move. Now ask yourself, are you a brown colt or a black colt. Remember, in either case you can still be promoted, but don't assume because you are the black colt you will be automatically promoted.

94.

THE SKUNK AND THE COLT

The colt had just finished working in the fields and was trotting to the farm where his master lived. Along the way, the colt was stopped by a skunk.

"Excuse me my tall friend. Would your master be interested in having me work for him? I could stop the deer from eating the corn in his field."

"How would you do that?"

"I would patrol the field at night and use my trusty tail to scare off any deer."

"I think that's a great idea. You're hired."

"Could you give me some food in advance, and I will pay it off with my first paycheck."

The colt stomps his hoof on the ground, "My master will give you 30 ears of corn as a loan. You start tonight."

A few weeks later, the colt was pulling a small wagon when he saw the skunk up ahead.

"Excuse me my young friend. Do you think your Master will <u>loan</u> me some corn seed so I may plant my own crops? I will gladly repay him once my crops come in."

"Hop in the wagon, I know where the corn seed is kept." The colt and skunk go to the barn to load the wagon and take it to the fields where the skunk will plant his crop.

The next day the colt is hard at work in the field with a plow behind him. At the edge of the field sits his friend, the skunk.

"Hello my strong friend. By chance could you help me plow my field so that I can plant my crop? Then I will be able to pay your master back as I promised."

"I would like to help but my master told me that you haven't earned your advance. He said many deer have been eating his crops and you haven't scared them away."

"I will start scaring the deer away tonight. If I do not plant the seed soon it will be too late because the season will be too short to grow the corn. If you plow my field, then once I sell my crops to the market, I will be happy to pay your master in cash."

"You'll pay in cash?"

"Yes."

"I'll help plow your fields."

"Could you do it now? I'm in a real hurry and I need it done quickly."

"I suppose I could put you ahead of this job." The colt began to plow the skunk's fields.

Summer had come and gone and no payments had been made. The Master wrote the skunk demanding payment for the seed. The skunk promised to pay. Fall came as quickly as summer. Again, the Master wrote the skunk about payment on the payroll advance, loan of seed and labor for the colt's plowing. The skunk had once promised to pay, but now began to say that the seed was not all good and would only make partial payment. The Master was angry at the skunk and knew the payment would not be made. When spring came and no payment had been made the Master called a trapper to catch the skunk to force him to pay or be skinned to pay off his debts.

> *A good customer is a paying customer.*

THE MORAL OF THE STORY

1. **Enforce credit limits.**
Armstrong has several inexperienced Armstrongers (colts) who allowed a customer (the skunk) to exceed its line of credit. This did not happen once, but on many occasions. The colts were always promised by the customer (the skunk), it would pay, but it never did. Every business sooner or later encounters customers who don't pay.

2. **Just because a customer is number one in sales does not give it the right to not pay.**
I have seen this happen many times especially with inexperienced Armstrongers. "But they're number one in sales for our company. We can't upset them. What can we do?" "Lose less money," I answer. A customer is no good, no matter how big they are, if they do not pay their bills.

3. **Watch the aging of accounts receivable.**
Thirty days late is better than 60, and 60 days late is better than 90. Catching the customer <u>early</u> will limit the amount of losses. If the customer owes you a lot of money, your decisions become more difficult to <u>enforce</u>. The more past due a customer becomes, typically the <u>larger</u> the dollar amount owed to your company. It's easy to write off a customer as a bad debt at $50,000, it's more difficult when it's $500,000.

ROOKIE STORYTELLERS

95.
ANOTHER CHRISTMAS CAROL

Several years ago in an attempt to help supplement our income, my wife, Maria, started babysitting in our home during the daytime. One day one of the children being cared for approached my wife with a request. The little five-year-old girl, Jessica, asked if she (my wife) would clean her glasses. My wife obliged. After a while, Jessica returned, asking Maria to perform the same task over. Again, Maria obliged and this time began to wonder why Jessica was concerned about her glasses being clean. A certain amount of time passed, and Jessica returned yet a third time with the very same request. Maria started cleaning Jessica's glasses, but this time she questioned the little girl. It seems Jessica was told by her parents that each time they found her glasses dirty, one of her Christmas gifts would be taken from her and given to a brother or sister.

Here's hoping everyone has a much more joyful Christmas season to look forward to than little Jessica did at that time.

You get more bees with honey than vinegar.

THE MORAL OF THE STORY

1. **A carrot on a stick.**
If we ever accomplish any of our goals by using negative means, think how much more can be accomplished using positive approaches. Perhaps Jessica might have been offered an extra gift (or reward) if she kept her glasses clean.

2. **The bottle is half full, not half empty.**
Human nature is negative, i.e., traffic lights are "stop" lights, gas tanks are always half "empty" instead of half full, etc. Christ knew this and taught against it. A wise minister once said that his daughter failed to arrive home at the 11:00 p.m. curfew with the family car. The next night he gave her the car keys and challenged her to see if she could get it right this time. She did and was not a repeat offender.

3. **Every gray cloud has a silver lining.**
Many companies feel it is necessary to discipline an employee with a negative reaction. After reading "The Seventh Commandment," a story by David Armstrong, I was impressed that apparently Armstrong tries to operate in a positive approach when confronted with problems surrounding an employee.

Rookie Storytellers

Authored by:
Michael W. Tribbett
Armstrong International, Inc., Michigan
and David M. Armstrong - 1995

96.
FIRST NAMES

I joined our company as its fifth employee in 1977. We were replacing the Department of Public Works, a government bureau similar to those which traditionally build and manage real estate for governments throughout North America. Many of the people we were hiring came from that Department and one of my many challenges as the company's "start-up" Human Resources Manager was to help create a culture which replicated a private company, rather than a government department.

There were about a dozen of us on the payroll in June of 1977. We were to grow to 1,213 people and come into full operation just 10 months later -- but that is the subject of many other stories. The first of our five Vice Presidents was John Davies who would be the only one to join us from the Government of British Columbia. John had hired a young secretary, Shelley Wilson, who had little experience, but all of it within the conservative, formal and somewhat stuffy government environment.

On the number of occasions that I passed Shelley or had something to talk with her about, she would always call me 'Mr. Kemp.' I had gently corrected her each time, telling her to call me Al, all to no avail. It was always, "John is out right now, Mr. Kemp," or "Thank you, Mr. Kemp."

One morning as I passed her desk, I said, "good morning, Shelley." The predictable, "Good morning, Mr.

Kemp," came back from her. I stopped short, turned on my heel, pointed my finger at her and in as stern a tone as I could muster, said, "If you call me Mr. Kemp one more time, I'll have John fire you!" Before she could react, I grinned from ear to ear, turned and walked away.

Shelley always called me Al from that day on and was an important ally in helping introduce an environment, which to this day, is known in part for its informality.

Armstrong International believes in using first names.

THE MORAL OF THE STORY

1. **Armstrong International believes in using first names.**
Only when customers are present should we use last names to show respect to Armstrong's management. I take it back. We should use our first names — that's who and what we are. Always use the last name for our visitors unless they prefer using their first names. They are not part of Armstrong's culture; they may not understand.

2. **Corporate culture is exceedingly important to a company's success** — but it doesn't just happen! Executives set, shape and change corporate culture. And they do it — knowingly or unknowingly — in the countless behaviors that they exhibit every minute of every day.

3. **Effective communications comes in part from our informal environment:**
"Al and Shelley" conversing is guaranteed to be more effective than "Mr. Kemp talking to Ms. Wilson."

4. **Once you've used someone's first name** . . . it's easier to become friends and work well together.

> Rookie Storytellers, Al Kemp
> V.P. Operations, British Columbia Buildings Corp.
> David M. Armstrong - 1997

97.

ONE MATCH FIRE MAKING

Every fall in schoolyards, wood lots, or campgrounds around the country, you'll see groups of young boys in Boy Scout uniforms practicing fire making skills. One of the tests that new Scouts must pass is to light a fire using only one match.

You might ask why, especially in this day and age where BIC lighters, propane stoves, and lanterns are plentiful? Is this a skill that is needed today, and by extension, is Scouting still relevant as we head into the 21st century?

Listen closely as the Scoutmaster explains what the young Scouts must do, and watch closely as they go about putting into practice his teachings. You just might find out.

You'll see them first pick the right spot for their fires. It will be a protected area, sheltered from the wind. They'll then start gathering the materials; dry paper that they may have in their pockets or they see lying around, or dry birch bark. Next will come dead branches found at the bottom of cedar, spruce or pine trees. They are very dry, even when it is raining heavily. Finally, larger pieces of wood will be gathered.

Once all of the materials are gathered, you'll see them breaking the wood and starting to build their fires. Paper or birch bark goes in the middle, then the kindling (small cedar/spruce/pine twigs) will be placed on top, and then larger branches. In arranging the wood, care is taken to allow space for airflow. Remaining larger pieces will be kept on the side to be added once the fire has been started.

The moment of truth has arrived for each Scout to light their fire using only one match. Before doing so however, he makes sure there is no wind, and if there is, he'll rig up a little shelter. Next, he'll determine what piece of paper of birch bark he wants to light first. Then he strikes the match and lights the fire, kneeling close to the fire to blow a little to get the wood going. Then, he adds more twigs where the flame is and places large pieces of wood on top of the fire.

You'll finally see the smile of success on his face as he basks in the glow of the fire he has just made — using only one match.

THE MORAL OF THE STORY

1. **To succeed at anything we need to plan** . . .
Whether it be lighting a fire with one match, or going for a job interview, or making an important presentation to a prospective customer.

2. **We learn best when we are involved**, i.e., learning by doing.
If you are a leader follow this moral when training employees.

3. **Lessons learned in childhood last a lifetime.**
Do you use them at work?

Authored by
Robert Saggers
Saggers & Associates, Quebec, Canada
Rookie Storytellers

98.

A TRIP TO REMEMBER

A few years ago the young son of Steve LaFalce, Armstrong Pilot, had a trip to remember. During spring vacation from school he was lucky enough to go along on the company airplane for a four-day trip to Stuart, Florida. Young Frank and his dad enjoyed going to the beach, swimming in the motel pool, and soaking up the sunshine.

During the trip back to Kalamazoo, Michigan Frank became ill. Maybe it was too much sun and fun, or too much food; whatever the reason, he threw up. Then he did it again. And again. In all, Frank had eleven episodes of stomach emptying, beyond the point where there was anything left to empty.

What made this trip memorable? All the way home, Barbara Armstrong cared for young Frank as if he were one of her own grandsons. The sight of Armstrong's First Lady holding a sick boy and comforting him during a three and a half hour plane ride is a memory Steve will value always.

> *Joy means put Jesus first, others second, yourself third*
> *—Somebody's Grandmother*

THE MORAL OF THE STORY

1. **Get Real!**
Showing that we care, that we are real human beings, leaves more of an impression on our fellow workers than we can imagine.

2. **We are family. — Sister Sledge.**
The title of this song describes one way Armstrongers feel about their company. Armstrong demonstrates this in many ways. The people of Armstrong demonstrate it in the ways they treat one another. It starts at the top with the First Lady.

3. **They just bought our loyalty for life.**
Steve's loyalty is <u>earned</u> when he watches the selfless act of Barbara Armstrong as she cares for his son.

Steve LaFalce, Pilot
Armstrong International, Inc.
Rookie Storytellers

99.

ARMSTRONG STEAM UNIVERSITY

Some 30 pupils listen carefully to the educators before them. It is 1999 and the instructors carry on a tradition that has gone on since 1958—all in the hallowed halls of Armstrong Steam University. What makes this year different than past years for two well-educated steam salesmen—now, turned professor? It just so happens that they are both coming off of record sales years.

The pupils now depart after an informative one-day session at Armstrong University. One of the mighty professors, Brad Savage from Merlo Steam (a long-time representative for Armstrong International) is quick to point out that he had a personal-best record sales year in 1998 — not to mention he was also named Merlo's "Salesman of the Year." Rick Atkins (also from Merlo Steam) is quick to point out that he too, had another "great year."

"You know, I attribute my success to one simple thing," Brad stresses. "I can tell you what has made the difference for me in the last year...seminars at Armstrong University in Three Rivers." "My 1998 sales increased dramatically over 1997, and there is no question in my mind that it is due to the many seminars we have been conducting at Armstrong University."

Rick is also quick to point out that his sales have risen accordingly – primarily due to an "increased focus on staging seminars." "As long as I have been dealing with my customers, education has been a key factor in bringing in more business." "It has become a must for me over the last couple years."

To educate or not to educate?

THE MORAL OF THE STORY

1. **Knowledge is power.**
Brad and Rick see the importance of educating, and at the same time, building upon a key business relationship with their customers. How? By offering seminars once a month, year-round. Brad and Rick will educate 360 customers (30 per month over 12 months) at Armstrong Steam University between them. They view this as "360 opportunities" to build a key business relationship — hence, grow their sales accordingly.

2. **Since there is not the typical demand for steam in the summer months, things are usually slower in the steam energy business.**
However, Rick and Brad have viewed this as just one more golden opportunity to don their professor hats and fully utilize the resources that Armstrong University has to offer.

Rookie Storytellers
David Casterline
Director of Corporate Communications
Armstrong International

100.

FINDING FAULT

When business executives are late for meetings, or miss them entirely, the schedules of many employees are affected. Many top executives will search out one person responsible for their missing a meeting and "heads will roll."

Recently, the Armstrong company airplane was scheduled to bring COO David Armstrong, General Counsel Tom Morris, and Associate General Counsel June Adams to Kalamazoo for a series of meetings at the Three Rivers plant. Through a series of missed phone calls, and other lapses in communication, the plane did not arrive in Kalamazoo until too late on the day of the meeting. As a result, several hundred employees were inconvenienced.

Was anyone punished or "chewed out" as a result? Was a search for a guilty party begun? Did fur fly and heads roll? Maybe that would be the case at some companies, but that's not the way we do it at Armstrong.

> "...And only the Master shall blame."
> Rudyard Kipling

THE MORAL OF THE STORY

1. **Who's to blame?**
When people make mistakes at Armstrong we don't scurry to find out who was at fault so blame can be placed on the guilty person. We figure out the best way to fix things and go forward.

2. **Do not search for fault to affix blame.**
Instead, we learn from our mistakes. Top executives should use these opportunities to coach and educate employees. This is an essential ingredient in effective leadership.

3. **Become a coach and teacher for yourself as well as each other.**
Learn from your own mistakes.

Rookie Storyteller
Steve LaFalce
Chief Pilot, Armstrong International

TO BE CONTINUED

☐ copies of:
Chief Storytelling Officer *(Paperback)*
$16.00 USA; $20.00 Canada plus $4.95 postage & handling (Michigan residents add applicable sales tax)

☐ copies of:
ONCE TOLD, THEY'RE GOLD *(Paperback)*
$16.00 USA; $20.00 Canada plus $4.95 postage & handling (Michigan residents add applicable sales tax)

☐ copies of:
HOW TO TURN YOUR COMPANY'S PARABLES INTO PROFIT *(Paperback)*
$14.00 USA; $18.00 Canada plus $4.95 postage & handling (Michigan residents add applicable sales tax)

☐ copies of:
MANAGING BY STORYING AROUND
(Paperback)
(Best Seller-Taiwan)
$14.00 USA; $18.00 Canada plus $4.95 postage & handling (Michigan residents add applicable sales tax)

☐ copies of:
ONCE TOLD, THEY'RE GOLD
(Compact Disc)
$59.95 USA; $77.95 Canada plus $4.95 postage & handling (Michigan residents add applicable sales tax)

Prices and postage are subject to change without notice.

copies of:

☐ **HOW TO TURN YOUR COMPANY'S PARABLES INTO PROFIT** *(Compact Disc)*
$49.95 USA; $64.95 Canada plus $4.95 postage & handling (Michigan residents add applicable sales tax)

copies of:

☐ **MANAGING BY STORYING AROUND** *(Compact Disc)*
$39.95 USA; $52.95 Canada plus $4.95 postage & handling (Michigan residents add applicable sales tax)

copies of:

☐ **STORIES ABOUT HAVING FUN AND BOOSTING CREATIVITY** *(Video)*
$29.95 USA; $34.95 Canada plus $4.95 postage & handling (Michigan residents add applicable sales tax)

copies of:

☐ **STORIES ABOUT TRATITIONS, LEGENDS, CULTURE AND CHANGE** *(Video)*
$29.95 USA; $34.95 Canada plus $4.95 postage & handling (Michigan residents add applicable sales tax)

copies of:

☐ **STORIES TO INSPIRE SELF-MANAGEMENT** *(Video)*
$29.95 USA; $34.95 Canada plus $4.95 postage & handling (Michigan residents add applicable sales tax)

Prices and postage are subject to change without notice.

HOW TO ORDER:

Call: (269) 273-1415
Fax Purchase Order: (269) 279-5728
Website Order: http://www.e-armstrong.com

OR MAIL TO:

Armstrong International, Inc.
816 Maple St.
Three Rivers, MI 49093-2347

PAYMENT BY CREDIT CARD:

☐ Mastercard   ☐ Visa   ☐ American Express

☐ Check/Money Order (Payable to David Armstrong)

Account No.: _____

Expiration Date: _____/_____

Signature _____

CUSTOMER INFORMATION:

Name: _____

Address: _____

City: _____ State: _____ Zip _____

INDEX OF NAMES

A-B

Adams, June...318
Aesop..257
Aiden, Paddy.......................................62
Alfing, Brian......................................172
Alfing, Norman..................................172
Allen, Gracie.......................................42
Andretti, Adam......................................6
Andretti, Mario.....................................7
Aristotle..283
Armstrong, Adam......................255,269
Armstrong, Barbara..........266,270,314
Armstrong, Gus.................157,180,255,265
Armstrong, Lawrence........................255
Armstrong, Patrick............................255
Armstrong, Yvonne.............................79
Atkins, Rick.......................................316
Atwood, Janel....................................235
Baker, Chad..93
Barrett, Raymond..............................237
Base, Richard....................................167
Beach, James...............................98,107
Bellow, Joe..144
Bennett, Stan....................................133
Blasius, Jan...56
Blasius, Pam.......................................94
Blood, Gary.......................................220
Bloss, Doug.......................................193
Blossom, Frank.................................268
Boele, Sue...223
Boote, David.......................................21
Bowser, Frank...................................172
Boynton, Jeff.....................................271
Boynton, Terry..................................271
Bronstetter, Dan................................174
Bucholtz, James............................53,57

C-E

Casterline, David........................6,52,317
Churchill, Winston............................126
Cinderella...243
Clay, Joyce.........................133,196,229
Clay, Ken...271
Closset, Roger.............................76,237
Collins, David.....................................94
Conroy, Sandy....................................46
Cook, Jeff..235
Cooling, Hadyn.................................131
Coop, Harold.......................17,176,209
Cribbs, Doug.....................................235
Cummings, Carl................................128
Cummings, Brittany..........................127
Cummings, Lauren............................127
Cummings, Rex.................................128
Cupid..19
Cuttler, Dennis..................................196
Daugherty, Jim.....................49,191,262
Daugherty, Larry......................29,70,91
Davies, John.....................................309
Dawson, Mr..86
Dipple, Dan..35
Disney, Walt..........................47,50,270
Drumm, Bill......................................269
Duncan, Kathy....................................44
Dyer, Marsha....................................255
Dyer, Maxine....................................255
Dykstra, David...................................96
Easter Bunny....................................121
Edison, Thomas................................270
English, Don.......................................41

INDEX OF NAMES

F-H

Findlay, Dan.....................197
Fonner, Dan......................193
Ford, Gary.......................224
Ford, Henry.................252,270
Franklin, Benjamin.........22,115,170,194,257
Furey, Benjamin..................201
Furey, Jamie Lynn................201
Furey, Joshua....................201
Furey, Mike......................201
Furey, Sharon....................201
Gardner, Herb.....................50
Gates, Bill......................270
Gibson, Steve.................32,193
Gillem, Pat......................114
God.........................20,92,97
Greenhalgh, John...................3
Griffin, Etta.................2,256
Grubka, Tom.............49,91,133,213,217
Hagenbuch, Larry..................21
Hager, Eric....................35,78
Handy, Ken........................52
Hartman, Bill, Sr.................23
Hartman, Bill.................21,125
Hartman, David...................255
Hartman, Forrest.................255
Hartman, William.................255
Hathaway, Roger..................131
Havens, Mike.....................176
Hay, Steve........................21
Hines, Gail......................144
Hitz, Rich.......................118
Hoffman, Edna................208,229
Holliday, Paul...................131
Hooley, Brady....................188
Hooley, Shelby...................188
Horton, Bill......................49
Hradsky, Bob......................12
Huyck, Randy.....................252
Hyatt, Tom.....................29,93

J-L

Jackson, Andrew..................158
Jefferson, Thomas................170
Jesus.............................92
Jones, Tim..................29,46,93
Kain, Grant..................1,169,207
Kauffman, Charlie................255
Kauffman, Jeff...................255
Kaup, Marcia.....................235
Kealy, John......................193
Keech, David.....................157
Kemp, Al.........................309
King Arthur......................195
Kipling Rudyard..................318
Kipp, Reid.......................134
Kirchner, Bob.....................21
Kirchner, Ed..................2,146
Knight, Paul..................73,131
Knisely, Keith....................21
LaFalce, Frank...................314
LaFalce, Steve...............314,319
Lao-Tze...........................16
LeBeau, Rusty....................265
Leprechauns......................121
Lincoln, Abraham.................290
Loomis, Kim.......................21
Lucas, Kim...................188,211
Luttrell, Ron....................243

326 CORPORATE STORYTELLING OFFICER

INDEX OF NAMES

M-N

Marks, Roger	21
Mason, Nicole	46
Meany, Joe	131
Mencius	245
Miller, Tom	115
Minett, Roy	131
Mischa	83
Montanini, Elvia	237
Morrell, Michelle	129
Morris, Tom	96,318
Mother Teresa	26
Newbre, Fred	21,253
Newbre, Lester	255
Nimtz, Brian	32
Noble, Tom	133
North, Roy	131

O-P

O'Dell, Dave	21
Osterloh, Mike	142
Pasteur, Louis	36
Peter Pan	243
Peters, Roger	21
Peters, Tom	53,74,116,159,266
Phillips Kerry	172,226
Pickering, Mark	131
Pinocchio	242
Poland, Dan	78
Post, Marcia	202
Postman, Neil	121
Pratt, Keith	196

Q-S

Quake, Tom	117
Quirin, Mark	193
Reece, Diane	223
Reed, Pat	129,228
Reynolds, Charlie	152
Richardson, Don	167
Rockwell, Tom	117,131
Saggers, Robert	313
Samson, Lori	228
Santa Claus	121,127
Savage, Brad	316
Scare, Rex	26,46,93
Schlesch, Ron	76,177
Schull, Deb	129
Scott, Bob	199
Sealy, Donna	25,144
Sears, Corey	6
Sears, Kim	6
Shirk, Andy	272
Shorris, Earl	95
Shutler, Dave	120
Sister Sledge	315
Smith, Dr.	83
Somboon, Mr.	70
Sparks, Tom	15
Spence, Cam	33,91
Spencer, Kathy	212
Steamstrong, Armey	94
Stitch Fairies	121
Stuart, Kim	131

INDEX OF NAMES

T-V	
Tase, Warren	155
Terrance	112
Thorndale, Russell	131
Tinkerbell	43
Tisch, Matt	57
Tomlin, Lily	221
Tompkins, Miss	91
Tony The Tiger	87
Tooth Fairy	121
Torrans, Dan	191
Townsend, Robert	20
Tribbett, Maria	307
Tribbett, Michael	308
Ulmer, Mike	242
Van Scoik, Jack	246
Vazques, Janette	144
Vedmore, Willie	52,55,177
Verheul, Dick	244
Vogel, Chris	32,161

W-Z	
Wang, Renee	25
Warner, Stu	2
Webb, David	131
Welch, Greg	205
Wilson, Harry	268
Wilson, Shelley	309
Wilson, Warren	91
Wolfe, Mike	41
Wright, Leo	253
Wright, Perry	207
Wright, Richard	52,253
Yang, James	226
Ziegler, Robert	246